Workshop on Geometrical Models of Natural Language Semantics 2010

(GEMS 2010)

Held at ACL 2010

Uppsala, Sweden
16 July 2010

ISBN: 978-1-61738-816-3

Printed from e-media with permission by:

Curran Associates, Inc.
57 Morehouse Lane
Red Hook, NY 12571

Some format issues inherent in the e-media version may also appear in this print version.

Printed by Curran Associates, Inc. (2010)

For permission requests, please contact the Association for Computational Linguistics at the address below.

Association for Computational Linguistics
209 N. Eighth Street
Stroudsburg, Pennsylvania 18360

Phone: 1-570-476-8006
Fax: 1-570-476-0860

acl@aclweb.org

Additional copies of this publication are available from:

Curran Associates, Inc.
57 Morehouse Lane
Red Hook, NY 12571 USA
Phone: 845-758-0400
Fax: 845-758-2634
Email: curran@proceedings.com
Web: www.proceedings.com

Introduction

This volume includes the papers presented at the GEMS 2010 Workshop - Geometrical Models for Natural Language Semantics, held on the 16th July 2010, jointly with the Conference of the Association for Computational Linguistics, ACL 2010, and endorsed by SigLex and SigSem.

Distributional models and semantic spaces represent a core topic in contemporary computational linguistics for their impact on advanced tasks and on other knowledge fields (such as social science and the humanities). Semantic spaces based on simple contextual units have been early used in information retrieval, showing dramatic impact on accuracy and scalability of many tasks. Later on, more linguistically principled spaces have been introduced for large-scale natural language learning problems, such as the acquisition of lexical taxonomies, word sense discrimination, pattern acquisition and conceptual clustering. More recently, specialized distributional models have been successfully applied to solve complex NLP tasks such as question answering, textual entailment and sentiment analysis. Cutting-edge applications include the adoption of semantic spaces as models of rich lexical semantic resources (e.g. lexical networks and lexicalized meaning theories, as frame semantics), and of machine learning approaches based on kernel methods.

The GEMS 2010 Workshops builds on the successful first edition held in Athens in 2009 jointly with the Conference of the European Chapter of the Association for Computational Linguistics, which counted more than 40 registered people and a large audience. As a follow-up of the GEMS 2009 Workshop, the Special Issue of the *Journal of Natural Engineering* dedicated to "*Distributional Lexical Semantics*"[1] is a further proof of the high interest in this research area. The 2010 edition aims at consolidating GEMS' contribution to the field, by stimulating research on semantic spaces and distributional methods for NLP, by pushing for an interdisciplinary view, and by amplifying exchange of ideas, results and resources among often independent communities.

The Workshop has successfully gathered high quality contributions to problems of meaning representation, acquisition and use, including a total of 15 paper submissions. After a peer-review phase, the program committee has selected 8 papers to be presented at the workshop, all of which have been included in these proceedings. The papers are representative of the current state of the art in distributional semantics, including:

- cutting edge researches on geometric techniques and machine learning, such as tensor analysis, non-linear embeddings, kernel methods, and latent topic models;
- applications of semantic space models to lexical acquisition tasks;
- novel optimization techniques for efficient and scalable distributional methods.

We would like to thank all the authors for the hard work dedicated to the submissions, and the members of the program committee for their precious reviewing. A special thanks goes to Katrin Erk for her invited contribution that provides a challenging and inspiring vision on the topic. Finally, we acknowledge the ACL 2010 organization and mostly the workshop chairs, Pushpak Bhattacharyia and David Weir, for their constant support across all the preparatory work.

Roberto Basili, University of Roma, *Tor Vergata*, Italy
Marco Pennacchiotti, *Yahoo! Inc*, Sunnyvale, USA.

June, 2010

[1] http://art.uniroma2.it/jnle

Organizers:

Roberto Basili (University of Roma, Tor Vergata, Italy)
Marco Pennacchiotti, (Yahoo! Inc., Santa Clara, CA, US)

Program Committee:

Enrique Alfonseca (Google Research, US)
Marco Baroni (University of Trento, Italy)
Paul Buitelaar (DFKI, Germany)
John A. Bullinaria (University of Birmingham, UK)
Carlotta Domeniconi (George Mason University, US)
Katrin Erk (University of Texas, US)
Stefan Evert (University of Osnabruck, Germany)
Alfio Massimiliano Gliozzo (STLab - ISTC-CNR, Italy)
Gregory Grefenstette (Exalead S.A., France)
Alpa Jain (Yahoo! Labs, US)
Jussi Karlgren (Swedish Institute of Computer Science)
Alessandro Lenci (University of Pisa, Italy)
Alessandro Moschitti (University of Trento, Italy)
Sebastian Pado (Stanford University, US)
Ted Pedersen (University of Minnesota, US)
Yves Peirsman (University of Leuven, Belgium)
Ana-Maria Popescu (Yahoo! Labs, US)
Magnus Sahlgren (Swedish Institute of Computer Science, Sweden)
Sabine Schulte im Walde (University of Stuttgart, Germany)
Hristo Tanev (Yahoo! UK, UK)
Tim Van de Cruys (University of Groningen, The Netherlands)
Peter D. Turney (National Research Council, Canada)
Yorick Wilks (University of Sheffield, UK)
Fabio Massimo Zanzotto (University of Roma, Tor Vergata, Italy)

Invited Speaker:

Katrin Erk, University of Texas at Austin, US

Table of Contents

Capturing Nonlinear Structure in Word Spaces through Dimensionality Reduction
David Jurgens and Keith Stevens 1

Manifold Learning for the Semi-Supervised Induction of FrameNet Predicates: An Empirical Investigation
Danilo Croce and Daniele Previtali 7

(Invited Paper) *What Is Word Meaning, Really? (And How Can Distributional Models Help Us Describe It?)*
Katrin Erk 17

Relatedness Curves for Acquiring Paraphrases
Georgiana Dinu and Grzegorz Chrupala 27

A Regression Model of Adjective-Noun Compositionality in Distributional Semantics
Emiliano Guevara 33

Semantic Composition with Quotient Algebras
Daoud Clarke, Rudi Lutz and David Weir 38

Expectation Vectors: A Semiotics Inspired Approach to Geometric Lexical-Semantic Representation
Justin Washtell 45

Sketch Techniques for Scaling Distributional Similarity to the Web
Amit Goyal, Jagadeesh Jagaralamudi, Hal Daumé III and Suresh Venkatasubramanian 51

Active Learning for Constrained Dirichlet Process Mixture Models
Andreas Vlachos, Zoubin Ghahramani and Ted Briscoe 57

Workshop Program

July 16, 2010

9:25–9:30 Welcome and Opening

Session: Geometry and Semantics

9:30–10:00 *Capturing Nonlinear Structure in Word Spaces through Dimensionality Reduction*
David Jurgens and Keith Stevens

10:00–10:30 *Manifold Learning for the Semi-Supervised Induction of FrameNet Predicates: An Empirical Investigation*
Danilo Croce and Daniele Previtali

10:30–11:00 Coffee Break

Invited Talk

11:00–12:10 *What Is Word Meaning, Really? (And How Can Distributional Models Help Us Describe It?)*
Katrin Erk

Session: Lexical Acquisition (1)

12:10–12:40 *Relatedness Curves for Acquiring Paraphrases*
Georgiana Dinu and Grzegorz Chrupala

12:40–13:10 *A Regression Model of Adjective-Noun Compositionality in Distributional Semantics*
Emiliano Guevara

13:10–14:30 Lunch

July 16, 2010 (continued)

Session: Lexical Acquisition (2)

14:30–15:00 *Semantic Composition with Quotient Algebras*
Daoud Clarke, Rudi Lutz and David Weir

15:00–15:30 *Expectation Vectors: A Semiotics Inspired Approach to Geometric Lexical-Semantic Representation*
Justin Washtell

15:30–16:00 Coffee Break

Session: Computational Aspects

16:00–16:30 *Sketch Techniques for Scaling Distributional Similarity to the Web*
Amit Goyal, Jagadeesh Jagaralamudi, Hal Daumé III and Suresh Venkatasubramanian

16:30–17:00 *Active Learning for Constrained Dirichlet Process Mixture Models*
Andreas Vlachos, Zoubin Ghahramani and Ted Briscoe

Panel

17:00–17:55 GEMS panel

17:55–18:00 Closing Remarks

Capturing Nonlinear Structure in Word Spaces through Dimensionality Reduction

David Jurgens
University of California, Los Angeles,
4732 Boelter Hall
Los Angeles, CA 90095
jurgens@cs.ucla.edu

Keith Stevens
University of California, Los Angeles,
4732 Boelter Hall
Los Angeles, CA 90095
kstevens@cs.ucla.edu

Abstract

Dimensionality reduction has been shown to improve processing and information extraction from high dimensional data. Word space algorithms typically employ linear reduction techniques that assume the space is Euclidean. We investigate the effects of extracting nonlinear structure in the word space using Locality Preserving Projections, a reduction algorithm that performs manifold learning. We apply this reduction to two common word space models and show improved performance over the original models on benchmarks.

1 Introduction

Vector space models of semantics frequently employ some form of dimensionality reduction for improvement in representations or computational overhead. Many of the dimensionality reduction algorithms assume that the unreduced word space is linear. However, word similarities have been shown to exhibit many non-metric properties: asymmetry, e.g North Korea is more similar to Red China than Red China is to North Korea, and non-transitivity, e.g. Cuba is similar the former USSR, Jamaica is similar to Cuba, but Jamaica is not similar to the USSR (Tversky, 1977). We hypothesize that a non-linear word space model might more accurately preserve these non-metric relationships.

To test our hypothesis, we capture the nonlinear structure with dimensionality reduction by using Locality Preserving Projection (LPP) (He and Niyogi, 2003), an efficient, linear approximation of Eigenmaps (Belkin and Niyogi, 2002). With this reduction, the word space vectors are assumed to exist on a nonlinear manifold that LPP learns in order to project the vectors into a Euclidean space. We measure the effects of using LPP on two basic word space models: the Vector Space Model and a Word Co-occurrence model. We begin with a brief overview of these word spaces and common dimensionality reduction techniques. We then formally introduce LPP. Following, we use two experiments to demonstrate LPP's capacity to accurately dimensionally reduce word spaces.

2 Word Spaces and Reductions

We consider two common word space models that have been used with dimensionality reduction. The first is the Vector Space Model (VSM) (Salton et al., 1975). Words are represented as vectors where each dimension corresponds to a document in the corpus and the dimension's value is the number of times the word occurred in the document. We label the second model the Word Co-occurrence (WC) model: each dimension correspond to a unique word, with the dimension's value indicating the number of times that dimension's word co-occurred.

Dimensionality reduction has been applied to both models for three kinds of benefits: to improve computational efficiency, to capture higher order relationships between words, and to reduce noise by smoothing or eliminating noisy features. We consider three of the most popular reduction techniques and the general word space models to which they have been applied: linear projections, feature elimination and random approximations.

The most frequently applied linear projection technique is the Singular Value Decomposition (SVD). The SVD factors a matrix A, which represents a word space, into three matrices $U\Sigma V^\top$ such that Σ is a diagonal matrix containing the singular values of A, ordered descending based on their effect on the variance in the values of A. The original matrix can be approximated by using only the top k singular values, setting all others to 0. The approximation matrix, $\hat{A} = U_k \Sigma_k V_k^\top$, is the least squares best-fit rank-k approximation of A.

Proceedings of the 2010 Workshop on GEometrical Models of Natural Language Semantics, ACL 2010, pages 1–6,
Uppsala, Sweden, 16 July 2010.

The SVD has been used with great success on both models. Latent Semantic Analysis (LSA) (Landauer et al., 1998) extends the (VSM) by decomposing the space using the SVD and making the word space the left singular vectors, U_k. WC models have also utilized the SVD to improve performance (Schütze, 1992; Bullinaria and Levy, 2007; Baroni and Lenci, 2008).

Feature elimination reduces the dimensionality by removing those with low information content. This approach has been successfully applied to WC models such as HAL (Lund and Burgess, 1996) by dropping those with low entropy. This technique effectively removes the feature dimensions of high frequency words, which provide little discriminatory content.

Randomized projections have also been successfully applied to VSM models, e.g. (Kanerva et al., 2000) and WC models, e.g. (Sahlgren et al., 2008). This reduction statistically approximates the original space in a much lower dimensional space. The projection does not take into account the structure of data, which provides only a computational benefit from fewer dimensions, unlike the previous two reductions.

3 Locality Preserving Projection

For a set of vectors, $x_1, x_2, \ldots, x_n \in \mathbb{R}^m$, LPP preserves the distance in the k-dimensional space, where $k \ll m$, by solving the following minimization problem,

$$\min_{w} \sum_{ij} (\mathbf{w}^\top \mathbf{x}_i - \mathbf{w}^\top \mathbf{x}_j)^2 S_{ij} \qquad (1)$$

where $\mathbf{w}$ is a transformation vector that projects $\mathbf{x}$ into the lower dimensional space, and S is a matrix that represents the local structure of the original space. Minimizing this equation is equivalent to finding the transformation vector that best preserves the local distances in the original space according to S. LPP assumes that the data points $\mathbf{x}_i$ exist on a manifold. This is in contrast to the SVD, which assumes that the space is Euclidean and performs a global, rather than local, minimization. In treating the space as a manifold, LPP is able to discover some of the nonlinear structure of the data from its local structure.

To solve the minimization problem in Equation 1, LPP uses a linear approximation of the Laplacian Eigenmaps procedure (Belkin and Niyogi, 2002) as follows:

1. Let X be a matrix where $\mathbf{x}_i$ is the ith row vector. Construct an adjacency matrix, S, which represents the local structure of the original vector space, by making an edge between points $\mathbf{x}_i$ and $\mathbf{x}_j$ if $\mathbf{x}_j$ is locally proximate to $\mathbf{x}_i$. Two variations are available for determining proximity: either the k-nearest neighbors, or all the data points with similarity $> \epsilon$.
2. Weight the edges in S proportional to the closeness of the data points. Four main options are available: a Gaussian kernel, a polynomial kernel, cosine similarity, or binary.
3. Construct the diagonal matrix D where entry $D_{ii} = \sum_j S_{ij}$. Let $L = D - S$. Then solve the generalized eigenvector problem:

   $$XLX^\top \mathbf{w} = \lambda XDX^\top \mathbf{w}. \qquad (2)$$

   He and Niyogi (2003) show that solving this problem is equivalent to solving Equation 1.
4. Let $W_k = [\mathbf{w}_1, \ldots, \mathbf{w}_k]$ denote the matrix of transformation vectors, sorted in descending order according to their eigenvalues λ. The original space is projected into k dimensions by $W_k^\top X \rightarrow X_k$.

For many applications of LPP, such as document clustering (He et al., 2004), the original data matrix X is transformed by first performing Principle Component Analysis and discarding the smallest principle components, which requires computing the full SVD. However, for large data sets such as those frequently used in word space algorithms, performing the full SVD is computationally infeasible.

To overcome this limitation, Cai et al. (2007a) show how Spectral Regression may be used as an alternative for solving the same minimization equation through an iterative process. The principle idea is that Equation 2 may be recast as

$$S\mathbf{y} = \lambda D\mathbf{y} \qquad (3)$$

where $\mathbf{y} = X^\top \mathbf{w}$, which ensures $\mathbf{y}$ will be an eigenvector with the same eigenvalue for the problem in Equation 2. Finding the transformation matrix W_k, used in step 4, is done in two steps. First, Equation 3 is solved to produce eigenvectors $[\mathbf{y}_0, \ldots, \mathbf{y}_k]$, sorted in decreasing order according to their eigenvalues λ. Second, the set of transformation vectors composing W_k, $[\mathbf{w}_1, \ldots, \mathbf{w}_k]$, is found by a least-squares regression:

$$\mathbf{w}_j = \operatorname*{argmin}_{\mathbf{w}} \sum_{i=1}^{n} (\mathbf{w}^\top \mathbf{x}_i - \mathbf{y}_i^j)^2 + \alpha ||\mathbf{w}||^2 \qquad (4)$$

where $\mathbf{y}_i^j$ denotes the value of the jth dimension of $\mathbf{y}_i$. The α parameter penalizes solutions proportionally to their magnitude, which Cai et al. (2007b) note ensures the stability of $\mathbf{w}$ as an approximate eigenproblem solution.

4 Experiments

Two experiments measures the effects of nonlinear dimensionality reduction for word spaces. For both, we apply LPP to two basic word space models, the VSM and WC. In the first experiment, we measure the word spaces' abilities to model semantic relations, as determined by priming experiments. In the second experiment, we evaluate the representation capabilities of the LPP-reduced models on standard word space benchmarks.

4.1 Setup

For the VSM-based word space, we consider three different weighting schemes: no weighting, TF-IDF and the log-entropy (LE) used in (Landauer et al., 1998). For the WC-based word space, we use a 5 word sliding window. Due to the large parameter space for LPP models, we performed only a limited configuration search. An initial analysis using the 20 nearest neighbors and cosine similarity did not show significant performance differences when the number of dimensions was varied between 50 and 1000. We therefore selected 300 dimensions for all tests. Further work is needed to identify the impact of different parameters. Stop words were removed only for the WC+LPP model. We compare the LPP-based spaces to three models: VSM, HAL, and LSA.

Two corpora are used to train the models in both experiments. The first corpus, TASA, is a collection of 44,486 essays that are representative of the reading a student might see upon entering college, introduced by (Landauer et al., 1998). The corpus consists of 98,420 unique words; no filtering is done when processing this corpus. The second corpus, WIKI, is a 387,082 article subset of a December 2009 Wikipedia snapshot consisting of all the articles with more than 1,000 tokens. The corpus is filtered to retain the top 100,000 most frequent tokens in addition to all the tokens used in each experiment's data set.

4.2 Experiment 1

Semantic priming measures word association based on human responses to a provided cue. Priming studies have been used to evaluate word spaces by equating vector similarity with an increased priming response. We use data from two types of priming experiments to measure whether LPP models better correlate with human performance than non-LPP word spaces.

Normed Priming Nelson et al. (1998) collected free association responses to 5,019 prime words. An average of 149 participants responded to each prime with the first word that came to mind.

Based on this dataset, we introduce a new benchmark that correlates word space similarity with the associative strength of semantic priming pairs. We use three measures for modeling prime-target strength, which were inspired by Steyvers et al. (2004). Let W_{ab} be the percentage of participants who responded to prime a with target b. The three measures of associative strength are

$$S^1_{ab} = W_{ab}$$
$$S^2_{ab} = W_{ab} + W_{ba}$$
$$S^3_{ab} = S^2_{ab} + \sum_c S^2_{ac} S^2_{cb}$$

These measure three different levels of semantic relatedness between words a and b. S^1_{ab} measures the relationship from a to b, which is frequently asymmetric due to ordering, e.g. "orange" produces "juice" more frequently than "juice" produces "orange." S^2_{ab} measures the symmetric association between a and b; Steyvers et al. (2004) note that this may better model the associative strength by including weaker associates that may have been a suitable second response. S^3_{ab} further increases the association by including the indirect associations between a and b from all cued primes.

For each measure, we rank a prime's targets according to their strength and then compute the Spearman rank correlation with the prime-target similarities in the word space. The rank comparison measures how well word space similarity corresponds to the priming association. We report the average rank correlation of associational strengths over all primes.

Priming Effect The priming study by Hodgson (1991), which evaluated how different semantic relationships affected the strength of priming, provides the data for our second priming test. Six relationships were examined in the study: antonymy, synonymy, conceptual association (sleep and bed), categorical coordinates (mist and rain), phrasal associates (pony and express), and super- and subordinates. Each relationship contained an average

Algorithm	Antonymy R[b]	Antonymy U	Antonymy E	Conceptual R	Conceptual U	Conceptual E	Coordinates R	Coordinates U	Coordinates E
VSM+LPP+LE	0.103	0.018	0.085	0.197	0.050	0.147	0.071	0.027	0.044
VSM+LPP+TF-IDF	0.348	0.321	0.027	0.408	0.414	-0.005	0.323	0.294	0.029
VSM+LPP	0.247	0.122	0.124	0.312	0.120	0.193	0.230	0.111	0.119
VSM+LPP[a]	0.298	0.070	**0.228**	0.284	0.033	0.252	0.321	0.037	**0.284**
WC+LPP	0.255	0.071	0.185	0.413	0.110	0.303	0.431	0.134	**0.298**
HAL	0.813	0.716	0.096	0.845	0.814	0.031	0.861	0.809	0.052
HAL[a]	0.915	0.879	0.037	0.867	0.846	0.021	0.913	0.861	0.052
LSA	0.235	0.023	0.213	0.392	0.028	**0.364**	0.199	0.014	0.185
LSA[a]	0.287	0.061	0.226	0.362	0.041	0.321	0.316	0.037	0.278
VSM	0.051	0.011	0.040	0.111	0.012	0.099	0.032	0.008	0.024

Algorithm	Phrasal R	Phrasal U	Phrasal E	Ordinates R	Ordinates U	Ordinates E	Synonymy R	Synonymy U	Synonymy E
VSM+LPP+LE	0.147	0.039	0.108	0.225	0.032	0.193	0.081	0.027	0.053
VSM+LPP+TF-IDF	0.438	0.425	0.013	0.277	0.290	-0.013	0.344	0.328	0.017
VSM+LPP	0.234	0.107	0.127	0.273	0.115	0.158	0.237	0.157	0.080
VSM+LPP[a]	0.202	0.031	0.171	0.270	0.032	0.238	0.299	0.069	0.230
WC+LPP	0.274	0.087	0.186	0.324	0.076	0.248	0.345	0.111	0.233
HAL	0.805	0.776	0.029	0.825	0.789	0.036	0.757	0.681	0.076
HAL[a]	0.866	0.856	0.010	0.881	0.857	0.024	0.898	0.879	0.019
LSA	0.280	0.021	**0.258**	0.258	0.018	0.240	0.197	0.019	0.178
LSA[a]	0.269	0.030	0.238	0.326	0.032	**0.294**	0.327	0.052	**0.275**
VSM	0.104	0.013	0.091	0.061	0.008	0.053	0.052	0.009	0.043

[a] Processed using the WIKI corpus

[b] R are related primes, U are unrelated primes, E is the priming effect

Table 1: Experiment 1 priming results for the six relation categories from Hodgson (1991)

Algorithm	Corpus	Word Choice TOEFL	Word Choice ESL	Word Choice RDWP	Word Association F. et al.	Word Association R.&G.	Word Association Deese
VSM+LPP+le	TASA	24.000	50.000	45.313	0.296	0.092	0.034
VSM+LPP+tf-idf	TASA	22.667	25.000	37.209	0.023	0.086	0.001
VSM+LPP	TASA	41.333	**54.167**	39.063	0.219	0.136	0.045
VSM+LPP	Wiki	33.898	48.780	43.434	0.530	0.503	0.108
WC+LPP	TASA	46.032	40.000	45.783	0.423	0.414	0.126
HAL	TASA	44.00	20.83	50.00	0.173	0.180	0.318
HAL	Wiki	50.00	31.11	43.44	0.261	0.195	0.042
LSA	TASA	56.000	50.000	55.814	0.516	0.651	**0.349**
LSA	Wiki	60.759	**54.167**	59.200	**0.614**	**0.681**	0.206
VSM	TASA	**61.333**	52.083	**84.884**	0.396	0.496	0.200

Table 2: Results from Experiment 2 on six word space benchmarks

of 23 word pairs. Hodgson's results showed that priming effects were exhibited by the prime-target pairs in all six categories.

We use the same methodology as Padó and Lapata (2007) for this data set; the prime-target (Related Primes) cosine similarity is compared with the average cosine similarity between the prime and all other targets (Unrelated Primes) within the semantic category. The priming effect is the difference between the two similarity values.

4.3 Experiment 2

We use six standard word space benchmarks to test our hypothesis that LPP can accurately capture general semantic knowledge and association based relations. The benchmarks come in two forms: word association and word choice tests.

Word choice tests provide a target word and a list of options, one of which has the desired relation to the target. To answer these questions, we select the option with the highest cosine similarity with the target. Three word choice synonymy benchmarks are used: the Test of English as a Foreign Language (TOEFL) test set from (Landauer et al., 1998), the English as a Second Language (ESL) test set from (Turney, 2001), and the Canadian Reader's Digest Word Power (RDWP) from (Jarmasz and Szpakowicz, 2003).

Algorithm	Corpus	S^1	S^2	S^3
VSM+LPP+LE	TASA	0.457	0.413	0.255
VSM+LPP+TF-IDF	TASA	0.464	0.390	0.207
VSM+LPP	TASA	0.457	0.427	0.275
VSM+LPP	Wiki	0.472	0.440	0.333
WC+LPP	TASA	0.469	0.437	0.315
HAL	TASA	0.485	0.434	0.310
HAL	Wiki	0.462	0.406	0.266
LSA	TASA	**0.494**	**0.481**	**0.414**
LSA	Wiki	0.489	0.472	0.398
VSM	TASA	0.484	0.460	0.407

Table 3: Experiment 1 results for normed priming.

Word association tests measure the semantic relatedness of two words by comparing their similarity in the word space with human judgements. These tests are more precise than word choice tests because they take into account the specific value of the word similarity. Three word association benchmarks are used: the word similarity data set of Rubenstein and Goodenough (1965), the word-relatedness data set of Finkelstein et al. (2002), and the antonymy data set of Deese (1964), which measures the degree to which high similarity captures the antonymy relationship. The Finkelstein et al. test is notable in that the human judges were free to score based on any word relationship.

5 Results and Discussion

The LPP-based models show mixed performance in comparison to existing models on normed priming tasks, shown in Table 3. Adding LPP to the VSM decreased performance; however, when WIKI was used instead of TASA, the VSM+LPP model increased .15 on all correlations, whereas LSA's performance decreased. This suggests that LPP needs more data than LSA to properly model the word space manifold. WC+LPP performs comparably to HAL, which indicates that LPP is effective in retaining the original WC space's structure in significantly fewer dimensions.

For the categorical priming tests shown in Table 1, LPP-based models show competitive results. VSM+LPP with the WIKI corpus performs much better than other VSM+LPP configurations. Unlike in the previous priming experiment, adding LPP to the base models resulted in a significant performance improvement. We also note that both HAL models and the VSM+LPP+TF-IDF model have high similarity ratings for unrelated primes. We posit that these models' feature weighting results in poor differentiation between words in the same semantic category, which causes their decreased performance.

For experiment 2, LPP-based spaces showed mixed results on word choice benchmarks, while showing notable improvement on the more precise word association benchmarks. Table 2 lists the results. Notably, LPP-based spaces performed well on the ESL synonym benchmark but poorly on the TOEFL synonym benchmark, even when the larger WIKI corpus was used. This suggests that LPP was not effective in retaining the relationship between certain classes of synonyms. Given that performance did not improve with the WIKI corpus, further analysis is needed to identify whether a different representation of the local structure would improve results or if the poor performance is due to another factor. While LSA and VSM model performed best on all benchmarks, LPP-based spaces performed competitively on the word association tests. In all but two tests, the WC+LPP model outperformed HAL.

The results from both experiments indicate that LPP is capable of accurately representing distributional information in a much lower dimensional space. However, in many cases, applications using the SVD-reduced representations performed better. In addition, application of standard weighting schemes worsened LPP-models' performance, which suggests that the local neighborhood is adversely distorted. Nevertheless, we view these results as a promising starting point for further evaluation of nonlinear dimensionality reduction.

6 Conclusions and Future Work

We have shown that LPP is an effective dimensionality reduction technique for word space algorithms. In several benchmarks, LPP provided a significant benefit to the base models and in a few cases outperformed the SVD. However, it does not perform consistently better than existing models. Future work will focus on four themes: identifying optimal LPP parameter configurations; improving LPP with weighting; measuring LPP's capacity to capture higher order co-occurrence relationships, as was shown for the SVD (Lemaire et al., 2006); and investigating whether more computationally expensive nonlinear reduction algorithms such as ISOMAP (Tenenbaum et al., 2000) are better for word space algorithms. We plan to release implementations of the LPP-based models as a part of the S-Space Package (Jurgens and Stevens, 2010).

References

Marco Baroni and Alessandro Lenci. 2008. Concepts and properties in word spaces. *From context to meaning: Distributional models of the lexicon in linguistics and cognitive science (Special issue of the Italian Journal of Linguistics)*, 1(20):55–88.

Mikhail Belkin and Partha Niyogi. 2002. Laplacian Eigenmaps and Spectral Techniques for Embedding and Clustering. In *Advances in Neural Information Processing Systems*, number 14.

John A. Bullinaria and Joseph P. Levy. 2007. Extracting semantic representations from word co-occurrence statistics: a computational study. *Behavior Research Methods*, 39:510–526.

Deng Cai, Xiaofei He, and Jiawei Han. 2007a. Spectral regression for efficient regularized subspace learning. In *IEEE International Conference on Computer Vision (ICCV'07)*.

Deng Cai, Xiaofei He, Wei Vivian Zhang, , and Jiawei Han. 2007b. Regularized Locality Preserving Indexing via Spectral Regression. In *Proceedings of the 2007 ACM International Conference on Information and Knowledge Management (CIKM'07)*.

James Deese. 1964. The associative structure of some common english adjectives. *Journal of Verbal Learning and Verbal Behavior*, 3(5):347–357.

Lev Finkelstein, Evgeniy Gabrilovich, Yossi Matias, Ehud Rivlin, Zach Solan, Gadi Woflman, and Eytan Ruppin. 2002. Placing search in context: The concept revisited. *ACM Transactions of Information Systems*, 20(1):116–131.

Xiaofei He and Partha Niyogi. 2003. Locality preserving projections. In *Advances in Neural Information Processing Systems 16 (NIPS)*.

Xiaofei He, Deng Cai, Haifeng Liu, and Wei-Ying Ma. 2004. Locality preserving indexing for document representation. In *SIGIR '04: Proceedings of the 27th annual international ACM SIGIR conference on Research and development in information retrieval*, pages 96–103.

James M. Hodgson. 1991. Informational constraints on pre-lexical priming. *Language and Cognitive Processes*, 6:169–205.

Mario Jarmasz and Stan Szpakowicz. 2003. Roget's thesaurus and semantic similarity. In *Conference on Recent Advances in Natural Language Processing*, pages 212–219.

David Jurgens and Keith Stevens. 2010. The S-Space Package: An Open Source Package for Word Space Models. In *Proceedings of the ACL 2010 System Demonstrations*.

Pentti Kanerva, Jan Kristoferson, and Anders Holst. 2000. Random indexing of text samples for latent semantic analysis. In L. R. Gleitman and A. K. Josh, editors, *Proceedings of the 22nd Annual Conference of the Cognitive Science Society*, page 1036.

Thomas K. Landauer, Peter W. Foltz, and Darrell Laham. 1998. Introduction to Latent Semantic Analysis. *Discourse Processes*, (25):259–284.

Benoît Lemaire, , and Guy Henhiére. 2006. Effects of High-Order Co-occurrences on Word Semantic Similarities. *Current Psychology Letters*, 1(18).

Kevin Lund and Curt Burgess. 1996. Producing high-dimensional semantic spaces from lexical co-occrrence. *Behavoir Research Methods, Instruments & Computers*, 28(2):203–208.

Douglas L. Nelson, Cathy L. McEvoy, and Thomas A. Schreiber. 1998. The University of South Florida word association, rhyme, and word fragment norms. `http://www.usf.edu/FreeAssociation/`.

Sebastian Padó and Mirella Lapata. 2007. Dependency-Based Construction of Semantic Space Models. *Computational Linguistics*, 33(2):161–199.

Herbert Rubenstein and John B. Goodenough. 1965. Contextual correlates of synonymy. *Communications of the ACM*, 8:627–633.

Magnus Sahlgren, Anders Holst, and Pentti Kanerva. 2008. Permutations as a means to encode order in word space. In *Proceedings of the 30th Annual Meeting of the Cognitive Science Society (CogSci'08)*.

Gerard Salton, A. Wong, and C. S. Yang. 1975. A vector space model for automatic indexing. *Communications of the ACM*, 18(11):613–620.

Hinrich Schütze. 1992. Dimensions of meaning. In *Proceedings of Supercomputing '92*, pages 787–796.

Mark Steyvers, Richard M. Shiffrin, and Douglas L. Nelson, 2004. *Word association spaces for predicting semantic similarity effects in episodic memory*. American Psychological Assocation.

Joshua B. Tenenbaum, Vin de Silva, and John C. Langford. 2000. A global geometric framework for nonlinear dimensionality reduction. *Science*, 290(5500):2319–2323.

Peter D. Turney. 2001. Mining the Web for synonyms: PMI-IR versus LSA on TOEFL. In *Proceedings of the Twelfth European Conference on Machine Learning (ECML-2001)*, pages 491–502.

Amos Tversky. 1977. Features of similarity. *Psychological Review*, 84:327–352.

Manifold Learning for the Semi-Supervised Induction of FrameNet Predicates: An Empirical Investigation

Danilo Croce and **Daniele Previtali**
{croce,previtali}@info.uniroma2.it
Department of Computer Science, Systems and Production
University of Roma, *Tor Vergata*

Abstract

This work focuses on the empirical investigation of distributional models for the automatic acquisition of frame inspired predicate words. While several semantic spaces, both word-based and syntax-based, are employed, the impact of geometric representation based on dimensionality reduction techniques is investigated. Data statistics are accordingly studied along two orthogonal perspectives: Latent Semantic Analysis exploits global properties while Locality Preserving Projection emphasizes the role of local regularities. This latter is employed by embedding prior FrameNet-derived knowledge in the corresponding non-euclidean transformation. The empirical investigation here reported sheds some light on the role played by these spaces as complex kernels for supervised (i.e. Support Vector Machine) algorithms: their use configures, as a novel way to semi-supervised lexical learning, a highly appealing research direction for knowledge rich scenarios like FrameNet-based semantic parsing.

1 Introduction

Automatic Semantic Role Labeling (SRL) is a natural language processing (NLP) technique that maps sentences to semantic representations and identifies the semantic roles conveyed by sentential constituents (Gildea and Jurafsky, 2002). Several NLP applications have exploited this kind of semantic representation ranging from Information Extraction (Surdeanu et al., 2003; Moschitti et al., 2003)) to Question Answering (Shen and Lapata, 2007), Paraphrase Identification (Pado and Erk, 2005), and the modeling of Textual Entailment relations (Tatu and Moldovan, 2005). Large scale annotated resources have been used by Semantic Role Labeling methods: they are commonly developed using a supervised learning paradigm where a classifier learns to predict role labels based on features extracted from annotated training data. One prominent resource has been developed under the Berkeley FrameNet project as a semantic lexicon for the core vocabulary of English, according to the so-called $frame$ semantic model (Fillmore, 1985). Here, a frame is a conceptual structure modeling a prototypical situation, evoked in texts through the occurrence of its lexical units (LU) that linguistically expresses the situation of the frame. Lexical units of the same frame share semantic arguments. For example, the frame KILLING has lexical units such as *assassin, assassinate, blood-bath, fatal, murderer, kill* or *suicide* that share semantic arguments such as KILLER, INSTRUMENT, CAUSE, VICTIM. The current FrameNet release contains about 700 frames and 10,000 LUs. A corpus of 150,000 annotated examples sentences, from the British National Corpus (BNC), is also part of FrameNet.

Despite the size of this resource, it is under development and hence incomplete: several frames are not represented by evoking words and the number of annotated sentences is unbalanced across frames. It is one of the main reason for the performance drop of supervised SRL systems in out-of-domain scenarios (Baker et al., 2007) (Johansson and Nugues, 2008). The limited coverage of FrameNet corpus is even more noticeable for the LUs dictionary: it only contains 10,000 lexical units, far less than the 210,000 entries in WordNet 3.0. For example, the lexical unit *crown*, according to the annotations, evokes the ACCOUTREMENT frame. It refers to a particular sense: according to WordNet, it is "an ornamental jeweled headdress signifying sovereignty". According to the same lexical resource, this LU has 12 lexical senses and the first one (i.e. "The Crown

Proceedings of the 2010 Workshop on GEometrical Models of Natural Language Semantics, ACL 2010, pages 7–16,
Uppsala, Sweden, 16 July 2010.

(or the reigning monarch) as the symbol of the power and authority of a monarchy") could evoke other frames, like LEADERSHIP. In (Pennacchiotti et al., 2008) and (De Cao et al., 2008), the problem of LU automatic induction has been treated in a semi-supervised fashion. First, LUs are modeled by exploiting the distributional analysis of an unannotated corpus and the lexical information of WordNet. These representations were used in order to find out frames potentially evoked by novel words in order to extend the FrameNet dictionary limiting the effort of manual annotations.

In this work the distributional model of LUs is further developed. As in (Pennacchiotti et al., 2008), several word spaces (Pado and Lapata, 2007) are investigated in order to find the most suitable representation of the properties which characterize a frame. Two dimensionality reduction techniques are applied here in this context. *Latent Semantic Analysis* (Landauer and Dumais, 1997) uses the Singular Value Decomposition to find the best subspace approximation of the original word space, in the sense of minimizing the global reconstruction error projecting data along the directions of maximal variance. *Locality Preserving Projection* (He and Niyogi, 2003) is a linear approximation of the nonlinear Laplacian Eigenmap algorithm: its locality preserving properties allows to add a set of constraints forcing LUs that belong to the same frame to be near in the resulting space after the transformation. LSA performs a global analysis of a corpus capturing relations between LUs and removing the noise introduced by spurious directions. However it risks to ignore lexical senses poorly represented into the corpus. In (De Cao et al., 2008) external knowledge about LUs is provided by their lexical senses from a lexical resource (e.g WordNet). In this work, prior knowledge about the target problem is directly embedded into the space through the LPP transformation, by exploiting locality constraints. Then a Support Vector Machine is employed to provide a robust acquisition of lexical units combining global information provided by LSA and the local information provided by LPP into a complex kernel function.

In Section 2 related work is presented. In Sections 3 the investigated distributional model of LUs is presented as well as the dimensionality reduction techniques. Then, in Section 4 the experimental investigation and comparative evaluations are reported. Finally, in Section 5 we draw final conclusions and outline future work.

2 Related Work

As defined in (Pennacchiotti et al., 2008), LU induction is the task of assigning a generic lexical unit not yet present in the FrameNet database (the so-called *unknown LU*) to the correct frame(s). The number of possible classes (i.e. frames) and the multiple assignment problem make it a challenging task. LU induction has been integrated at SemEval-2007 as part of the Frame Semantic Structure Extraction shared task (Baker et al., 2007), where systems are requested to assign the correct frame to a given LU, even when the LU is not yet present in FrameNet. Several approaches show low coverage (Johansson and Nugues, 2007) or low accuracy, like (Burchardt et al., 2005). This task is presented in (Pennacchiotti et al., 2008) and (De Cao et al., 2008), where two different models which combine distributional and paradigmatic (i.e. lexical) information have been discussed. The distributional model is used to select a list of frame suggested by the corpus' evidences and then the plausible lexical senses of the unknown LU are used to re-rank proposed frames.

In order to exploit prior information provided by the frame theory, the idea underlying is that semantic knowledge can be embedded from external sources (i.e the FrameNet database) into the distributional model of unannotated corpora. In (Basu et al., 2006) a limited prior knowledge is exploited in several clustering tasks, in term of pairwise constraints (i.e., pairs of instances labeled as belonging to same or different clusters). Several existing algorithms enhance clustering quality by applying supervision in the form of constraints. These algorithms typically utilize the pairwise constraints to either modify the clustering objective function or to learn the clustering distortion measure. The approach discussed in (Basu et al., 2006) employs Hidden Markov Random Fields (HMRFs) as a probabilistic generative model for semi-supervised clustering, providing a principled framework for incorporating constraint-based supervision into prototype-based clustering.

Another possible approach is to directly embed the prior-knowledge into data representations. The main idea is to employ effective and efficient algorithms for constructing nonlinear low-dimensional manifolds from sample data points embedded in high-dimensional spaces. Several algorithms are defined, including Isometric feature mapping (ISOMAP) (Tenenbaum et al., 2000), Locally Linear Embedding (LLE) (Roweis and Saul, 2000), Local Tangent Space alignment (LTSA) (Zhang and Zha, 2004) and Locality Preserving Projection (LPP) (He and Niyogi, 2003) and they have been successfully applied in several computer vision and pattern recognition problems. In (Yang et al., 2006) it is demonstrated that basic nonlinear dimensionality reduction algorithms, such as LLE, ISOMAP, and LTSA, can be modified by taking into account prior information on exact mapping of certain data points. The sensitivity analysis of these algorithms shows that prior information improves stability of the solution. In (Goldberg and Elhadad, 2009), a strategy to incorporate lexical features into classification models is proposed. Another possible approach is the strategy pursued in recent works on deep learning techniques to NLP tasks. In (Collobert and Weston, 2008) a unified architecture for NLP that learns features relevant to the tasks at hand given very limited prior knowledge is presented. It embodies the idea that a multitask learning architecture coupled with semi-supervised learning can be effectively applied even to complex linguistic tasks such as Semantic Role Labeling. In particular, (Collobert and Weston, 2008) proposes an embedding of lexical information using Wikipedia as source, and exploits the resulting language model for the multitask learning process. The extensive use of unlabeled texts allows to achieve a significant level of lexical generalization in order to better capitalize on the smaller annotated data sets.

3 Geometrical Embeddings as models of Frame Semantics

The aim of this distributional approach is to model frames in semantic spaces where words are represented from the distributional analysis of their co-occurrences over a corpus. Semantic spaces are widely used in NLP for representing the meaning of words or other lexical entities. They have been successfully applied in several tasks, such as information retrieval (Salton et al., 1975) and harvesting thesauri (Lin, 1998). The fundamental intuition is that the meaning of a word can be described by the set of textual contexts in which it appears (*Distributional Hypothesis* as described in (Harris, 1964)), and that words with similar vectors are semantically related. Contexts are words appearing together with a LU: such a space models a generic notion of semantic relatedness, i.e. two LUs spatially close in the space are likely to be either in paradigmatic or syntagmatic relation as in (Sahlgren, 2006). Here, LUs delimit subspaces modeling the prototypical semantic of the corresponding evoked frames and novel LUs can be induced by exploiting their projections.

Since a semantic space supports the language in use from the corpus statistics in an unsupervised fashion, vectors representing LUs can be characterized by different distributions. For example, LUs of the frame KILLING, such as *bloodbath*, *crucify* or *fratricide*, are statistically inferior in a corpus if compared to a wide-spanning term as *kill*. Moreover other ambiguous LUs, as *liquidate* or *terminate*, could appear in sentences evoking different frames. These problems of data-sparseness and distribution noise can be overcome by applying space transformation techniques augmenting the space expressiveness in modeling frame semantics. Semantic space models very elegantly map words in vector spaces (there are as many dimensions as words in the dictionary) and LUs collections into distributions of data-points. Every distribution implicitly expresses two orthogonal facets: global properties, as the occurrence scores computed for terms across the entire collection (irrespectively from their word senses or evoking situation) and local regularities, for example the existence of subsets of terms that tend to be used every time a frame manifests. These also tend to be closer in the space and should be closer in the transformed space too. Another important aspect that a transformation could account is external semantic information. In the new space, prior knowledge can be exploited to gather a more regular LUs representation and a clearer separation between subspaces representing different frame semantics.

In the following sections the investigated distributional model of LUs will be discussed. As many criteria can be adopted to define a LU context, one of the goals of this investigation is to find a co-occurrence model that better captures the notion of frames, as described in Section 3.1. Then, two dimensionality reduction techniques, exploiting semantic space distributions to improve frames representation, are discussed. In Section 3.2 the role of global properties of data statistics will be investigated through the Latent Semantic Analysis while in Section 3.3 the Locality Preserving Projection algorithm will be discussed in order to combine prior knowledge about frames with local regularities of LUs obtained from text.

3.1 Choosing the space

Different types of context define spaces with different semantic properties. Such spaces model a generic notion of *semantic relatedness*. Two LUs close in the space are likely to be related by some type of generic semantic relation, either paradigmatic (e.g. synonymy, hyperonymy, antonymy) or syntagmatic (e.g. meronymy, conceptual and phrasal association), as observed in (Sahlgren, 2006). The target of this work is the construction of a space able to capture the properties which characterize a frame, assuming those LUs in the same frame tend to be either co-occurring or substitutional words (e.g. *murder/kill*). Two traditional word-based co-occurrence models capture the above property:

Word-based space: Contexts are words, as lemmas, appearing in a n-window of the LU. The window width n is a parameter that allows the space to capture different aspects of a frame: higher values risk to introduce noise, since a frame could not cover an entire sentence, while lower values lead to sparse representations.

Syntax-based space: Contexts words are enriched through information about syntactic relations (e.g. *X-VSubj-killer* where *X* is the LU), as described in (Pado and Lapata, 2007). Two LUs close in the space are likely to be in a paradigmatic relation, i.e. to be close in an IS-A hierarchy (Budanitsky and Hirst, 2006; Lin, 1998). Indeed, as contexts are syntactic relations, targets with the same part of speech are much closer than targets of different types.

3.2 Latent Semantic Analysis

Latent Semantic Analysis (LSA) is an algorithm presented in (Furnas et al., 1988) afterwards diffused by Landauer (Landauer and Dumais, 1997): it can be seen as a variant of the Principal Component Analysis idea. LSA aims to find the best subspace approximation to the original word space, in the sense of minimizing the global reconstruction error projecting data along the directions of maximal variance. It captures term (semantic) dependencies by applying a matrix decomposition process called Singular Value Decomposition (SVD). The original term-by-term matrix M is transformed into the product of three new matrices: U, S, and V so that $M = USV^T$. Matrix M is approximated by $M_l = U_l S_l V_l^T$ in which only the first l columns of U and V are used, and only the first l greatest singular values are considered. This approximation supplies a way to project term vectors into the l-dimensional space using $Y_{terms} = U_l S_l^{1/2}$. Notice that the SVD process accounts for the eigenvectors of the entire original distribution (matrix M). LSA is thus an example of a decomposition process strongly dependent on a global property. The original statistical information about M is captured by the new l-dimensional space which preserves the global structure while removing low-variant dimensions, i.e. distribution noise. These newly derived features may be thought of as artificial concepts, each one representing an emerging meaning component as a linear combination of many different words (i.e. contexts). Such contextual usages can be used instead of the words to represent texts. This technique has two main advantages. First, the overall computational cost of the model is reduced, as similarities are computed on a space with much fewer dimensions. Secondly, it allows to capture second-order relations among LUs, thus improving the quality of the similarity measure.

3.3 The Locality Preserving Projection Method

An alternative to LSA, much tighter to local properties of data, is the Locality Preserving Projection (LPP), a linear approximation of the non-linear Laplacian Eigenmap algorithm introduced in (He and Niyogi, 2003). LPP is a linear dimensionality reduction method whose goal is, given a set of LUs $x_1, x_2, .., x_m$ in R^n, to find a transformation matrix A that maps these m points into a set of points $y_1, y_2, .., y_m$ in R^k ($k \ll n$). LPP achieves this result through a cascade of processing steps described hereafter.

Construction of an Adjacency graph. Let G denote a graph with m nodes. Nodes *i* and *j* have got a weighted connection if vectors x_i and x_j are close, according to an arbitrary measure of similarity. There are many ways to build an adjacency graph. The *cosine* graph with cosine weighting scheme is explored: given two vectors x_i and x_j, the weight w_{ij} between them is set by

$$w_{ij} = max\{0, \frac{cos(x_i, x_j) - \tau}{|cos(x_i, x_j) - \tau|} \cdot cos(x_i, x_j)\} \quad (1)$$

where a cosine threshold τ is necessary. The adjacency graph can be represented by using a symmetric $m \times m$ adjacency matrix, named W, whose element W_{ij} contains the weight between nodes i and j. The method of constructing an adjacency graph outlined above is correct if the data actually lie on a low dimensional manifold. Once such an adjacency graph is obtained, LPP will try to optimally preserve it in choosing projections.

Solve an Eigenmap problem. Compute the eigenvectors and eigenvalues for the generalized eigenvector problem:

$$XLX^T\mathbf{a} = \lambda XDX^T\mathbf{a}$$

where X is a $n \times m$ matrix whose columns are the original m vectors in R^n, D is a diagonal $m \times m$ matrix whose entries are column (or row) sums of W, $D_{ii} = \sum_j W_{ij}$ and $L = D - W$ is the Laplacian matrix. The solution of this problem is the set of eigenvectors $\mathbf{a}_0, \mathbf{a}_1, .., \mathbf{a}_{n-1}$, ordered according to their eigenvalues $\lambda_0 < \lambda_1 < .. < \lambda_{n-1}$. LPP projection matrix A is obtained by selecting the k eigenvectors corresponding to the k smallest eigenvalues: therefore it is a $n \times k$ matrix whose columns are the selected n-dimensional k eigenvectors. Final projection of original vectors into R^k can be linearly performed by $Y = A^T X$. This transformation provides a valid kernel that can be efficiently embedded into a classifier.

Embedding predicate knowledge through LPPs. While LSA finds a projection, according to the global properties of the space, LPP tries to preserve the local structures of the data. LPP exploits the adjacency graph in order to represent neighborhood information. It computes a transformation matrix which maps data points into a lower dimensional subspace. As the construction of an adjacency graph G can be based on any principle, its definition could account on some external information reflecting prior knowledge available about the task.

In this work, prior knowledge about LUs is embedded by exploiting their membership to frame dictionaries, thus removing from the graph all connections between LUs x_i and x_j that do not evoke the same prototypical situation. More formally Equation 1 can be rewritten more formally as:

$$w_{ij} = max\{0, \frac{cos(x_i, x_j) - \tau}{|cos(x_i, x_j) - \tau|} \cdot cos(x_i, x_j) \cdot \delta(i,j)\}$$

where

$$\delta(i,j) = \begin{cases} 1 & \textbf{iff } \exists F \; s.t. \; LU_i \in F \wedge LU_j \in F \\ 0 & \text{otherwise} \end{cases}$$

so the resulting manifold keeps close all LUs evoking the same frame. Since the number of connections could introduce too many constraints to the Eigenmap problem, a threshold is introduced to avoid the space collapse: for each LU, only the most-similar c connections are selected. The adoption of the proper *a priori* knowledge about the target task can be thus seen as a promising research direction.

4 Empirical Analysis

In this section the empirical evaluation of distributional models applied to the task of inducing LUs is presented. Different spaces obtained through the dimensionality reduction techniques imply different kernel functions used to independently train different SVMs. Our aim is to investigate the impact of these kernels in capturing both the frames and LUs' properties, as well as the effectiveness of their possible combination.

The problem of LUs' induction is here treated as a multi-classification problem, where each LU is considered as a positive or negative instance of a frame. We use Support Vector Machines (SVMs), (Joachims, 1999) a maximum-margin classifier that realizes a linear discriminative model. In case of not linearly separable examples, convolution functions $\phi(\cdot)$ can be used in order to transform the initial feature space into another one, where a hyperplane that separates the data with the widest margin can be found. Here new similarity measures, the kernel functions, can be defined through the dot-product $K(o_i, o_j) = \langle\phi(o_i) \cdot \phi(o_j)\rangle$ over the new representation. In this way, kernel functions K_{LSA} and K_{LPP} can be induced through the dimensionality reduction techniques ϕ_{LSA} and ϕ_{LPP} respectively, as described in sections 3.2 and 3.3. Kernel methods are advantageous because the combination of of kernel functions can be integrated into the SVM as they are still kernels. Consequently, the kernel combination $\alpha K_{LSA} + \beta K_{LPP}$ linearly combines the global properties captured by LSA and the locality constraints imposed by the LPP transformation. Here, parameters α and β weight the combination of the two kernels. The evoking frame for a novel LU is the one whose corresponding SVM has the highest (possibly negative) margin, according to a *one-*

	train	tune	test	overall
max	107	35	34	176
avg	28	8	8	44
total	2466	722	723	3911

Table 1: Number of LU examples for each data set from the 100 frames

vs-all scheme. In order to evaluate the quality of the presented models, accuracy is measured as the percentage of LUs that are correctly re-assigned to their original (gold-standard) frame. As the system can suggest more than one frame, different accuracy levels can be obtained. A LU is *correctly assigned* if its correct frame (according to FrameNet) belongs to the set of the best b proposals by the system (i.e. the first b scores from the underlying SVMs). Assigning different values to b, we obtained different levels of accuracy as the percentage of LUs that is correctly assigned among the first b proposals, as shown in Table 3.

4.1 Experimental Setup

The adopted gold standard is a subset of the FrameNet database and it consists of the most 100 represented frames in term of annotated examples and LUs. As the number of example is extremely unbalanced across frames[1], the LUs dictionary of each selected frame contains at least 10 LUs. It is a reasonable amount of information for the SVMs training and it is still a representative data set, being composed of 3,911 LUs, i.e. the 55% of the entire dictionary[2] of 7,230 evoking words. All word spaces are derived from the British National Corpus (BNC), which is underlying FrameNet and consisting of about 100 million words for English. Each selected frame is represented into the BNC by at least 362 annotated sentences, as the lack of a reasonable number of examples hardly produces a good distributional model of LUs. Each frame's list of LUs is split into train (60%), tuning (20%) and test set (20%) and LUs having Part-of-speech different from verb, noun or adjective are removed. In Table 1 the number of LUs for each set, as well as the maximum and the average number per frame, are summarized.

Four different approaches for the Word Space construction are used. The first two correspond to a Word-Based space, the last to a Syntax-Based, as described in section 3.1:

Window-*n* (W*n*): contextual features correspond to the set of the 20,000 most frequent lemmatized words in the BNC. The association measure between LUs and contexts is the Point-wise Mutual Information (PMI). Valid contexts for LUs are fixed to a n-window. Hereafter two window width values will be investigated: *Window5* (*W5*) and *Window10* (*W10*).

Sentence (Sent): contextual features are the same above, but the valid contexts are extended to the entire sentence length.

SyntaxBased (SyntB): contextual features have been computed according to the "dependency-based" vector space discussed[3] in (Pado and Lapata, 2007). Observable contexts here are made of syntactically-typed co-occurrences within dependency graphs built from the entire set of BNC sentences. The most frequent 20,000 basic features, i.e. (syntactic relation,lemma) pairs, have been employed as contextual features corresponding to PMI scores. Syntactic relations are extracted using the Minipar parser.

Word space models thus focus on the LUs of the selected 100 frames and the dimensionality have been reduced by applying LSA and LPP at a new size of $l = 100$. Any prior knowledge information is provided to the tuning and test sets during the LPP transformation: the construction of the reduced feature space takes in account only LUs from the train set while remaining predicates are represented through the LPP linear projection. In these experiments the cosine threshold τ and the maximum number of constraints c are estimated over the tuning set and the best parametrizations are shown in Table 2. The adopted implementation of SVM is SVM-Light-TK [4].

4.2 Results

In these experiments the impact of the lexical knowledge gathered by different word-spaces is evaluated over the LU induction task. Moreover, the improvements achieved through LSA and LPP is measured. SVM classifiers are trained over the semantic spaces produced through the dimension-

[1]For example the SELF_MOTION frame counts 6,248 examples while 119 frames are represented by less than 10 examples

[2]The entire database contains 10,228 LUs and the number of evoking word is 7,230, without taking in account multiple frame assignments.

[3]The `Minimal` context provided by the Dependency Vectors tool is used. It is available at http://www.nlpado.de/~sebastian/dv.html

[4]SVM-Light-TK is available at the url http://disi.unitn.it/~moschitt/Tree-Kernel.htm

	α/β											τ	c
	1.0/0.0	.9/.1	.8/.2	.7/.3	.6/.4	.5/.5	.4/.6	.3/.7	.2/.8	.1/.9	0.0/1.0		
$W5$	0.668	0.669	0.672	**0.673**	0.669	0.662	0.649	0.632	0.612	0.570	0.033	0.55	5
$W10$	0.615	**0.619**	0.618	0.612	0.604	0.597	0.580	0.575	0.565	0.528	0.048	0.65	3
$Sent$	0.557	0.567	0.580	**0.584**	0.574	0.564	0.561	0.545	0.523	0.496	0.048	0.80	5
$SyntB$	0.654	**0.664**	0.662	0.652	0.651	0.647	0.649	0.634	0.627	0.592	0.056	0.40	3

Table 2: Accuracy at different combination weights of kernel $\alpha K_{LSA} + \beta K_{LPP}$ (specific baseline is 0.043)

	b-1	b-2	b-3	b-4	b-5	b-6	b-7	b-8	b-9	b-10	α/β
$W5_{orig}$	0,563	0,685	0,733	0,770	0,801	0,835	0,841	0,854	0,868	0,879	-
$W10_{orig}$	0,510	0,634	0,707	0,776	0,810	0,830	0,841	0,857	0,865	0,875	-
$Sent_{orig}$	0,479	0,618	0,680	0,734	0,764	0,793	0,813	0,837	0,845	0,852	-
$SyntB_{orig}$	0,585	0,741	0,803	0,840	0,866	0,874	0,886	0,903	0,907	0,913	-
$W5_{LSA+LPP}$	**0.673**	0.781	0.831	**0.865**	**0.881**	0.891	**0.906**	**0.912**	**0.926**	**0.938**	0.7/0.3
$W10_{LSA+LPP}$	0.619	0.739	0.786	0.818	0.849	0.865	0.878	0.888	0.901	0.909	0.9/0.1
$Sent_{LSA+LPP}$	0.584	0.705	0.766	0.798	0.825	0.835	0.848	0.864	0.876	0.889	0.7/0.3
$SyntB_{LSA+LPP}$	0.664	**0.791**	**0.840**	0.864	0.878	**0.893**	0.901	0.903	0.907	0.911	0.9/0.1

Table 3: Accuracy of original word-space models (*orig*) and semantic space models (*LSA+LPP*) on best-k proposed frames

ality reduction transformations. Representations of both semantic spaces are linearly combined as $\alpha K_{LSA} + \beta K_{LPP}$, where kernel weights α and β are estimated over the tuning set. Both kernels are used even without a combination: a ratio $\alpha = 1.0/\beta = 0.0$ denotes the LSA kernel alone, while $\alpha = 0.0/\beta = 1.0$ the LPP kernel. Table 2 shows best results, obtained through a RBF kernel. The $Window5$ model achieves the highest accuracy, i.e. 67% of correct classification, where a baseline of 4.3% is estimated assigning LUs to the most likely frame in the training set (i.e. the one containing the highest number of LUs). Wider windows achieve lower classification accuracy confirming that most of lexical information tied to a frame is near the LU. The Syntactic-based word space does not outperform the accuracy of a word-based space. The combination of both kernels has always provided the best outcome and the LSA space seems to be more accurate and expressive respect to the LPP one, as shown in Figure 1. In particular LPP alone is extremely unstable, suggesting that constraints imposed by the prior knowledge are orthogonal with respect to the corpus statistics.

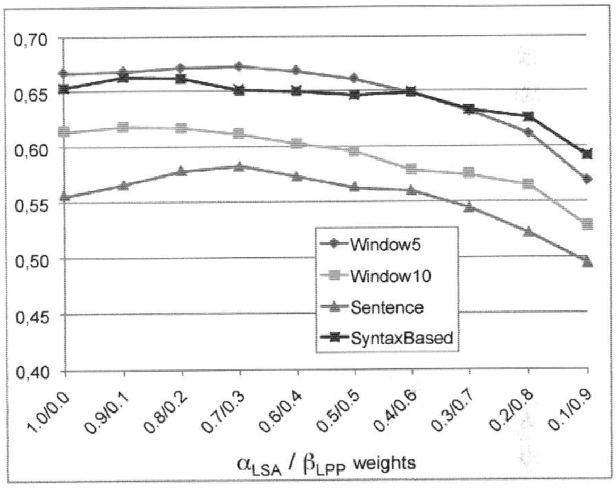

Figure 1: Accuracy at different combination weights of kernel $\alpha K_{LSA} + \beta K_{LPP}$

Further experiments are carried out using the original co-occurrence space models, to assess improvements due to LSA and LPP kernel. In the latter investigation linear kernel achieved best results as confirmed in (Bengio et al., 2005), where the sensitivity to the curse of dimensionality of a large class of modern learning algorithms (e.g. SVM) based on local kernels (e.g. RBF) is argued. As shown in Table 3, the performance drop of original (*orig*) models against the best kernel combination of LSA and LPP are significant, i.e. $\sim 10\%$, showing how the latent semantic spaces better capture properties of frames, avoiding data-sparseness, dimensionality problem and low-regularities of data-distribution.

Moreover, Table 3 shows how the accuracy level largely increases when more than one frame is considered: at a level $b = 3$, i.e. the novel LU is correctly classified if one of the original frames is comprised in the list (of three frames) proposed by the system, accuracy is 0.84 (i.e the SyntaxBased model), while at $b = 10$ accuracy is

LU (# WN_{syns})	frame_1	frame_2	frame_3	Correct frames
boil.v (5)	FOOD	FLUIDIC_MOTION	CONTAINERS	CAUSE_HARM
clap.v (7)	SOUNDS	MAKE_NOISE	COMMUNICATION_NOISE	BODY_MOVEMENT
crown.n (12)	LEADERSHIP	**ACCOUTREMENTS**	PLACING	ACCOUTREMENTS OBSERVABLE_BODYPARTS
school.n (7)	**EDUCATION_TEACHING**	BUILDINGS	**LOCALE_BY_USE**	EDUCATION_TEACHING LOCALE_BY_USE AGGREGATE
threat.n (4)	HOSTILE_ENCOUNTER	IMPACT	**COMMITMENT**	COMMITMENT
tragedy.n (2)	**TEXT**	KILLING	EMOTION_DIRECTED	TEXT

Table 4: Proposed 3 frames for each LU (ordered by SVM scores) and correct frames provided by the FrameNet dictionary. In parenthesis the number of different WordNet lexical senses for each LU.

nearly 0.94 (i.e Window5). It is high enough to support tasks such as the semi-automatic creation of new FrameNets. An error analysis indicates that many misclassifications are induced by a lack in the frame annotations, especially those concerning polysemic LUs[5]. Table 4 reports the analysis of a LU subset where the first 3 frames proposed for each evoking word are shown, ranked by the margin of the SMVs. The last column contains the frames evoked by LUs, according to the FrameNet dictionary, and the frame names in bold suggest their correct classification. Some LUs, like *threat* (characterized by 4 lexical senses) seem to be misclassified: in this case the FrameNet annotation regards a specific sense that evokes the COMMITMENT frame (e.g. "There was a real *threat* that she might have to resign") without taking in account other senses like WordNet's "menace, threat (something that is a source of danger)" that could evoke the HOSTILE_ENCOUNTER frame. In other cases proposed frames seem to enrich the LUs dictionary, like BUILDINGS, here evoked by *school*.

5 Conclusions

The core purpose of this was to present an empirical investigation of the impact of different distributional models on the lexical unit induction task. The employed word-spaces, based on different co-occurrence models (either context and syntax-driven), are used as vector models of the LU semantics. On these spaces, two dimensionality reduction techniques have been applied. Latent Semantic Analysis (LSA) exploits global properties of data distributions and results in a global model for lexical semantics. On the other hand, the Locality Preserving Projection (LPP) method, that exploits regularities in the neighborhood of each lexical predicate, is also employed in a semi-supervised manner: local constraints expressing prior knowledge on frames are defined in the adjacency graph. The resulting embedding is therefore expected to determine a new space where regions for LU of a given frame can be more easily discovered. Experiments have been run using the resulting spaces for task dependent kernels in a SVM learning setting. The application of the FrameNet KB on the 100 best represented frames showed that a combined use of the global and local models made available by LSA and LPP, respectively, achieves the best results, as the 67.3% of LUs recovers the same frames of the annotated dictionary. This is a significant improvement with respect to previous results achieved by the pure distributional model reported in (Pennacchiotti et al., 2008).

Future work is required to increase the level of constraints made available from the semi-supervised setting of LPP: syntactic information, as well as role-related evidence, can be both accommodated by the adjacency constraints imposed for LPP. This constitutes a significant area of research towards a comprehensive semi-supervised model of frame semantics, entirely based on manifold learning methods, of which this study on LSA and LPP is just a starting point.

Acknowledgement We want to acknowledge Prof. Roberto Basili because this work would not exist without his ideas, inspiration and invaluable support.

References

Collin Baker, Michael Ellsworth, and Katrin Erk. 2007. Semeval-2007 task 19: Frame semantic structure extraction. In *Proceedings of SemEval-2007*,

[5] According to WordNet, in our dataset an average of 3.6 lexical senses for each LU is estimated.

pages 99–104, Prague, Czech Republic, June. Association for Computational Linguistics.

Sugato Basu, Mikhail Bilenko, Arindam Banerjee, and Raymond Mooney. 2006. Probabilistic semi-supervised clustering with constraints. In *Semi-Supervised Learning*, pages 73–102. MIT Press.

Yoshua Bengio, Olivier Delalleau, and Nicolas Le Roux. 2005. The curse of dimensionality for local kernel machines. Technical report, Departement d'Informatique et Recherche Operationnelle.

Alexander Budanitsky and Graeme Hirst. 2006. Evaluating WordNet-based measures of semantic distance. *Computational Linguistics*, 32(1):13–47.

Aljoscha Burchardt, Katrin Erk, and Anette Frank. 2005. A WordNet Detour to FrameNet. In *Sprachtechnologie, mobile Kommunikation und linguistische Resourcen*, volume 8 of *Computer Studies in Language and Speech*. Peter Lang, Frankfurt/Main.

Ronan Collobert and Jason Weston. 2008. A unified architecture for natural language processing: deep neural networks with multitask learning. In *In Proceedings of ICML '08*, pages 160–167, New York, NY, USA. ACM.

Diego De Cao, Danilo Croce, Marco Pennacchiotti, and Roberto Basili. 2008. Combining word sense and usage for modeling frame semantics. In *In Proceedings of STEP 2008, Venice, Italy.*

Charles J. Fillmore. 1985. Frames and the semantics of understanding. *Quaderni di Semantica*, 4(2):222–254.

G. W. Furnas, S. Deerwester, S. T. Dumais, T. K. Landauer, R. A. Harshman, L. A. Streeter, and K. E. Lochbaum. 1988. Information retrieval using a singular value decomposition model of latent semantic structure. In *Proc. of SIGIR '88*, New York, USA.

Daniel Gildea and Daniel Jurafsky. 2002. Automatic labeling of semantic roles. *Computational Linguistics*, 28(3):245–288.

Yoav Goldberg and Michael Elhadad. 2009. On the role of lexical features in sequence labeling. In *In Proceedings of EMNLP '09*, pages 1142–1151, Singapore.

Zellig Harris. 1964. Distributional structure. In Jerrold J. Katz and Jerry A. Fodor, editors, *The Philosophy of Linguistics*, New York. Oxford University Press.

Xiaofei He and Partha Niyogi. 2003. Locality preserving projections. In *Proceedings of NIPS03*, Vancouver, Canada.

T. Joachims. 1999. *Making large-Scale SVM Learning Practical.* MIT Press, Cambridge, MA.

Richard Johansson and Pierre Nugues. 2007. Using WordNet to extend FrameNet coverage. In *Proceedings of the Workshop on Building Frame-semantic Resources for Scandinavian and Baltic Languages, at NODALIDA*, Tartu, Estonia, May 24.

Richard Johansson and Pierre Nugues. 2008. The effect of syntactic representation on semantic role labeling. In *Proceedings of COLING*, Manchester, UK, August 18-22.

Tom Landauer and Sue Dumais. 1997. A solution to plato's problem: The latent semantic analysis theory of acquisition, induction and representation of knowledge. *Psychological Review*, 104.

Dekang Lin. 1998. Automatic retrieval and clustering of similar word. In *Proceedings of COLING-ACL*, Montreal, Canada.

Alessandro Moschitti, Paul Morarescu, and Sanda M. Harabagiu. 2003. Open domain information extraction via automatic semantic labeling. In *FLAIRS Conference*, pages 397–401.

Sebastian Pado and Katrin Erk. 2005. To cause or not to cause: Cross-lingual semantic matching for paraphrase modelling. In *Proceedings of the Cross-Language Knowledge Induction Workshop*, Cluj-Napoca, Romania.

Sebastian Pado and Mirella Lapata. 2007. Dependency-based construction of semantic space models. *Computational Linguistics*, 33(2):161–199.

Marco Pennacchiotti, Diego De Cao, Roberto Basili, Danilo Croce, and Michael Roth. 2008. Automatic induction of framenet lexical units. In *Proceedings of The Empirical Methods in Natural Language Processing (EMNLP 2008) Waikiki, Honolulu, Hawaii.*

S.T. Roweis and L.K. Saul. 2000. Nonlinear dimensionality reduction by locally linear embedding. *Science*, 290(5500):2323–2326.

Magnus Sahlgren. 2006. *The Word-Space Model.* Ph.D. thesis, Stockholm University.

G. Salton, A. Wong, and C. Yang. 1975. A vector space model for automatic indexing. *Communications of the ACM*, 18:613Äì620.

Dan Shen and Mirella Lapata. 2007. Using semantic roles to improve question answering. In *Proceedings of EMNLP-CoNLL*, pages 12–21, Prague.

Mihai Surdeanu, , Mihai Surdeanu, A Harabagiu, John Williams, and Paul Aarseth. 2003. Using predicate-argument structures for information extraction. In *In Proceedings of ACL 2003.*

Marta Tatu and Dan I. Moldovan. 2005. A semantic approach to recognizing textual entailment. In *HLT/EMNLP*.

J. B. Tenenbaum, V. Silva, and J. C. Langford. 2000. A Global Geometric Framework for Nonlinear Dimensionality Reduction. *Science*, 290(5500):2319–2323.

Xin Yang, Haoying Fu, Hongyuan Zha, and Jesse Barlow. 2006. Semi-supervised nonlinear dimensionality reduction. In *23rd International Conference on Machine learning*, pages 1065–1072, New York, NY, USA. ACM Press.

Zhenyue Zhang and Hongyuan Zha. 2004. Principal manifolds and nonlinear dimensionality reduction via tangent space alignment. *SIAM J. Scientific Computing*, 26(1):313–338.

What Is Word Meaning, Really?
(And How Can Distributional Models Help Us Describe It?)

Katrin Erk
Department of Linguistics
University of Texas at Austin
katrin.erk@mail.utexas.edu

Abstract

In this paper, we argue in favor of reconsidering models for word meaning, using as a basis results from cognitive science on human concept representation. More specifically, we argue for a more flexible representation of word meaning than the assignment of a single best-fitting dictionary sense to each occurrence: Either use dictionary senses, but view them as having fuzzy boundaries, and assume that an occurrence can activate multiple senses to different degrees. Or move away from dictionary senses completely, and only model similarities between individual word usages. We argue that distributional models provide a flexible framework for experimenting with alternative models of word meanings, and discuss example models.

1 Introduction

Word sense disambiguation (WSD) is one of the oldest problems in computational linguistics (Weaver, 1949) and still remains challenging today. State-of-the-art performance on WSD for WordNet senses is at only around 70-80% accuracy (Edmonds and Cotton, 2001; Mihalcea et al., 2004). The use of coarse-grained sense groups (Palmer et al., 2007) has led to considerable advances in WSD performance, with accuracies of around 90% (Pradhan et al., 2007). But this figure averages over lemmas, and the problem remains that while WSD works well for some lemmas, others continue to be tough.

In WSD, polysemy is typically modeled through a list of dictionary senses thought to be mutually disjoint, such that each occurrence of a word is characterized through one best-fitting dictionary sense. Accordingly, WSD is typically framed as a classification task. Interestingly, the task of assigning a single best word sense is very hard for human annotators, not just machines (Kilgarriff and Rosenzweig, 2000).

In this paper we advocate the exploration of alternative computational models of word meaning. After all, one possible reason for the continuing difficulty of (manual as well as automatic) word sense assignment is that the prevailing model might be suboptimal. We explore three main hypotheses. The first builds on research on the human concept representation that has shown that concepts in the human mind do not work like sets with clear-cut boundaries; they show graded membership, and there are typical members as well as borderline cases (Rosch, 1975; Hampton, 2007). Accordingly, **(A)** we will suggest that **word meaning may be better modeled using a graded notion of sense membership** than through concepts with hard boundaries. Second, even if senses have soft boundaries, the question remains of whether they are disjoint. **(B)** We will argue in favor of a framework where **multiple senses may apply to a single occurrence, to different degrees**. This can be viewed as a dynamical grouping of senses for each occurrence, in contrast to static sense groups as in Palmer et al. (2007). The first two hypotheses still rely on an existing sense list. However, there is no universal agreement across dictionaries and across tasks on the number of senses that words have (Hanks, 2000). Kilgarriff (1997) even argues that general, task-independent word senses do not exist. **(C) By focusing on individual occurrences (usages) of a lemma and their degree of similarity, we can model word meaning without recourse to dictionary senses.**

In this paper, we are going to argue in favor of the use of vector space as a basis for alternative models of word meaning. Vector space models have been used widely to model word sense (Lund

Proceedings of the 2010 Workshop on GEometrical Models of Natural Language Semantics, ACL 2010, pages 17–26,
Uppsala, Sweden, 16 July 2010.

and Burgess, 1996; Deerwester et al., 1990; Landauer and Dumais, 1997; Sahlgren and Karlgren, 2005; Padó and Lapata, 2007), their central property being that proximity in space can be used to predict semantic similarity. By viewing word occurrences as points in vector space, we can model word meaning without recourse to senses. An additional advantage of vector space models is that they are also widely used in human concept representation models, yielding many modeling ideas that can be exploited for computational models.

In Section 2 we review the evidence that word sense is a tough phenomenon to model, and we lay out findings that support hypotheses (A)-(C). Section 4 considers distributional models that represent word meaning without recourse to dictionary senses, following (C). In Section 5 we discuss possibilities for embedding dictionary senses in vector space in a way that respects points (A) and (B).

2 Computational and cognitive models of word meaning

In this section, we review the problems of (manual and automatic) sense assignment, and we discuss discusses cognitive models of concept representation and polysemy, following the three hypotheses laid out in the introduction.

Word sense assignment. In computational linguistics, the problem of polysemy is typically phrased as one of choosing one best-fitting sense for the given occurrence out of a dictionary-defined sense list. However, this is a hard task both for humans and for machines. With WordNet (Fellbaum, 1998), the electronic lexicon resource that is currently most widely used in computational linguistics, inter-annotator agreement (ITA) lies in the range of 67% to 78% (Landes et al., 1998; Snyder and Palmer, 2004; Mihalcea et al., 2004), and state-of-the-art WSD systems achieve accuracy scores of 73% to 77% (Edmonds and Cotton, 2001; Mihalcea et al., 2004). This problem is not specific to WordNet: Analyses with the HECTOR dictionary led to similar numbers (Kilgarriff and Rosenzweig, 2000). Sense granularity has been suggested as a reason for the difficulty of the task (Palmer et al., 2007). And in fact, the use of more coarse-grained senses leads to greatly ITA as well as WSD accuracy, with about a 10% improvement for either measure (Palmer et al., 2007; Pradhan et al., 2007). In OntoNotes (Hovy et al., 2006), an ITA of 90% is used as the criterion for the construction of coarse-grained sense distinctions. However, intriguingly, for some high-frequency lemmas such as *leave* this ITA threshold is not reached even after multiple re-partitionings of the semantic space (Chen and Palmer, 2009) – indicating that the meaning of these words may not be separable into senses distinct enough for consistent annotation. A recent analysis of factors influencing ITA differences between lemmas (Passonneau et al., 2010) found three main factors: sense concreteness, specificity of the context in which a target word occurs, and similarity between senses. It is interesting to note that only one of those factors, the third, can be addressed through a change of dictionary.

More radical solutions than sense grouping that have been proposed are to restrict the task to determining predominant sense in a given domain (McCarthy et al., 2004), or to work directly with paraphrases (McCarthy and Navigli, 2009).

(A) Graded sense membership. Research on the human concept representation (Murphy, 2002; Hampton, 2007) shows that categories in the human mind are not simply sets with clear-cut boundaries. Some items are perceived as more typical than others (Rosch, 1975; Rosch and Mervis, 1975). Also, some items are clear members, others are rated as borderline (Hampton, 1979). On borderline items, people are more likely to change their mind about category membership (McCloskey and Glucksberg, 1978). However, these results concern mental concepts, which raises the question of the relation between mental concepts and word senses. This relation is discussed in most depth by Murphy (1991; 2002), who argues that while not every human concept is associated with a word, word meanings show many of the same phenomena as concepts in general; word meaning is "made up of pieces of conceptual structure". In cognitive linguistics there has been much work on word meaning based on models with graded membership and typically effects (Coleman and Kay, 1981; Lakoff, 1987; Cruse, 1986; Taylor, 1989).

(B) Multiple senses per occurrence. While most manual word sense annotation efforts allow annotators to assign more than one dictionary sense to an occurrence, this is typically phrased as an exception rather than the default. In the recent WSsim annotation study (Erk et al., 2009),

Sentence	Senses 1	2	3	4	5	6	7	Annotator
This question provoked **arguments** in America about the Norton Anthology of Literature by Women, some of the contents of which were said to have had little value as literature.	1	4	4	2	1	1	3	Ann. 1
	4	5	4	2	1	1	4	Ann. 2
	1	4	5	1	1	1	1	Ann. 3

Table 1: From (Erk et al., 2009): A sample annotation from the WSsim dataset. The senses are: 1:statement, 2:controversy, 3:debate, 4:literary argument, 5:parameter, 6:variable, 7:line of reasoning

we asked three human annotators to judge the applicability of WordNet senses on a graded scale of 1 (*completely different*) to 5 (*identical*) and giving a rating for *each* sense rather than picking one. Table 1 shows an example sentence with annotator ratings for the senses of the target *argument*. For this sentence, the annotators agree that senses 2 and 3 are highly applicable, but there also individual differences in the perceived meaning: Only annotator 2 views sense 1 as applying to a high degree. In an annotation setting with graded judgments, it does not make sense to measure exact agreement on judgments. We instead evaluated ITA using Spearman's rho, a nonparametric correlation test, finding highly significant correlations ($p \ll 0.001$) between each pair of annotators, as well as highly significant correlations with the results of a previous, traditional word sense annotation of the same dataset. The annotators made use of the complete scale (1-5), often opting for intermediate values of sense applicability. In addition, we tested whether there were groups of senses that always got the same ratings on any given sentence (which would mean that the annotators implicitly used more coarse-grained senses). What we found instead is that the annotators seemed to have mixed and matched senses for the individual occurrences in a dynamic fashion.

(C) Describing word meaning without dictionary senses. In lexicography, Kilgarriff (1997) and Hanks (2000) cast doubt on the existence of task-independent, distinct senses. In cognitive science, Kintsch (2007) calls word meaning "fluid and flexible". And some researchers in lexical semantics have suggested that word meanings lie on a continuum between clear cut cases of ambiguity on the one hand, and on the other hand vagueness where clear cut boundaries do not hold (Tuggy, 1993). There are some psychological studies on whether different senses of a polysemous word are represented separately in the mind or whether there is some joint representation. However, so far the evidence is inconclusive and varies strongly with the experimental setting. Some studies found evidence for a separate representation (Klein and Murphy, 2001; Pylkkanen et al., 2006). Brown (2008) finds a linear change in semantic similarity effects with sense distance, which could possibly point to a continuous representation of word meaning without clear sense boundaries. But while there is no definitive answer yet on the question of the mental representation of polysemy, a computational model that does not rely on distinct senses has the advantage of making fewer assumptions. It also avoids the tough lexicographic problem mentioned above, of deciding on a best set of senses for a given domain.

1) We study the methods and concepts that each writer uses to defend the cogency of legal, deliberative, or more generally political prudence against explicit or implicit charges that practical thinking is merely a knack or form of cleverness.

2) Eleven CIRA members have been convicted of criminal charges and others are awaiting trial.

Figure 1: From (Erk et al., 2009): A sense pair from the USim dataset, for the target *charge.n*. Annotator judgments: 2,3,4

In the recent USim annotation study (Erk et al., 2009), we tested whether human annotators could reliably and consistently provide word meaning judgments without the use of dictionary senses. Three annotators rated the similarity of pairs of occurrences (usages) of a common target word, again on a scale of 1-5. Figure 1 shows an example, with the corresponding annotator judgments. The results on this task were encouraging: Again using correlation to measure ITA, we found a highly significant correlation ($p \ll 0.001$) between the judgments of each pair of annotators. Furthermore, there was a strong correlation on judgments given with and without the use of dictionary senses (USim versus WSsim) for the same data.

3 Vector space models of word meaning in isolation

This section gives a brief overview of the use of vector spaces to model concepts and word meaning in cognition and computational linguistics.

In two of the current main theories of concept representation, feature vectors play a prominent role. Prototype theory (Hampton, 1979; Smith and Medin, 1981) models degree of category membership through similarity to a single prototype. Exemplar models (Medin and Schaffer, 1978; Nosofsky, 1992; Nosofsky and Palmeri, 1997) represent a concept as a collection of all previously seen exemplars and compute degree of category membership as similarity to stored exemplars. Both prototypes and exemplars are typically represented as feature vectors. Many models represent a concept as a region rather than a point in space, often characterized by a feature vector plus a separate dimension weight vector (Smith et al., 1988; Hampton, 1991; Gärdenfors, 2004). The features are individually meaningful and interpretable and include sensory and motor features as well as function and taxonomic features. There are several datasets with features elicited from human subjects (McRae et al., 2005; Vigliocco et al., 2004).

In computational linguistics, distributional models represent the meaning of a word as a vector in a high-dimensional space whose dimensions characterize the contexts in which the word typically occurs (Lund and Burgess, 1996; Landauer and Dumais, 1997; Sahlgren and Karlgren, 2005; Padó and Lapata, 2007). In the simplest case, the dimensions are context words, and the values are co-occurrence counts. In contrast to spaces used in cognitive science, the dimensions in distributional models are typically not interpretable (though see Almuhareb and Poesio (2005), Baroni et al. (2010)). A central property of distributional models is that proximity in vector space is a predictor of semantic similarity. These models have been used successfully in NLP (Deerwester et al., 1990; Manning et al., 2008), as well as in psychology (Landauer and Dumais, 1997; Lowe and McDonald, 2000; McDonald and Ramscar, 2001).

4 Vector space models of word meaning in context

If we want to represent word meaning through individual usages and their similarity only, without the use of dictionary senses (along hypothesis (C)), distributional models are an obvious choice, if we can just represent each individual usage as a point in space. However, vector space models have mostly been used to represent the meaning of a word in isolation: The vector for a word is computed by summing over all its corpus occurrences, thereby summing over all its meanings. There are a few vector space models of meaning *in context*, though they differ in what it is that they model. One group of models computes a single vector for a whole sentence, encoding both the words and the syntactic structure (Smolensky, 1990; B. Coecke and Clark, 2010). In this case, the dimensionality of the vectors varies with the syntactic complexity of the sentence in question. A second group also computes a single vector for a whole expression, but the vector for a larger expression is a combination of the word vectors for the words occurring in the expression (Landauer and Dumais, 1997; Mitchell and Lapata, 2008). Syntactic structure is not encoded. The resulting vector, of the same dimensionality as the word vectors, is then a combination of the contexts in which the words of the sentence occur. A third group of approaches derives a separate vector for each word in a given sentence (Erk and Padó, 2008; Thater et al., 2009; Erk and Padó, 2010). While an approach of the second type would derive a single, joint vector for, say, the expression *catch a ball*, an approach from the third group would derive two vectors, one for the word *catch* in the context of *ball*, and one for the word *ball* in the context of *catch*. In this third group, the dimensionality of a vector for a word in context is the same as for a word in isolation.

In this paper, we focus on the third type of approaches. Our aim is to study alternatives to dictionary senses for characterizing word meaning. So we need a meaning characterization for each individual word in a given sentence context, rather than a single vector for a larger expression.

We can also classify distributional approaches to word meaning in context into *prototype-* and *exemplar-based* approaches. Prototype-based approaches first compute a (prototype) vector for each word in isolation, then modify this vector according to the context in a given occurrence (Landauer and Dumais, 1997; Mitchell and Lapata, 2008; Erk and Padó, 2008; Thater et al., 2009). Typical methods for combining prototype vectors are addition, component-wise multiplication (introduced by Mitchell and Lap-

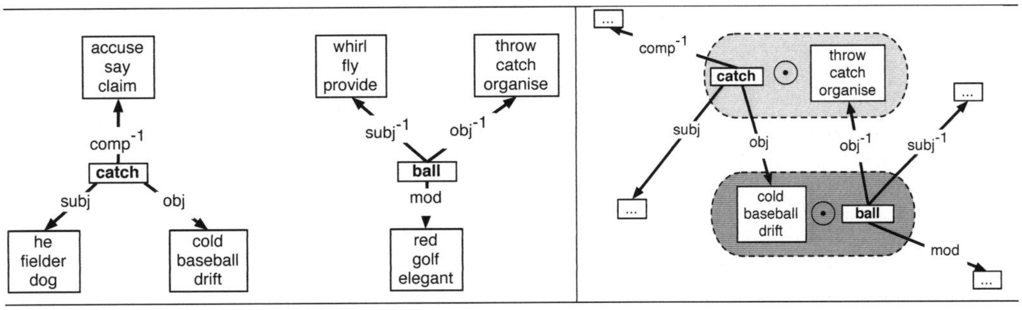

Figure 2: From (Erk and Padó, 2008): Left: Vector representations for verb *catch* and noun *ball.* Lexical information plus selectional preferences. Right: Computing context-specific meaning by combining predicate and argument via selectional preference vectors

ata (2008)), and component-wise minimum. Then there are *multiple prototype* approaches that statically cluster synonyms or occurrences to induce word senses(Schütze, 1998; Pantel and Lin, 2002; Reisinger and Mooney, 2010). *Exemplar-based* approaches represent a word in isolation as a collection of its occurrences or paraphrases, then select only the contextually appropriate exemplars for a given occurrence context (Kintsch, 2001; Erk and Padó, 2010). In this paper we focus on the first and third group of approaches, as they do not rely on knowledge of how many word senses (clusters) there should be.

A structured vector space model for word meaning in context. In Erk and Padó (2008), we proposed the *structured vector space model (SVS)*, which relies solely on syntactic context for computing a context-specific vector. It is a prototype-based model, , and called *structured* because it explicitly represents argument structure, using multiple vectors to represent each word. Figure 2 (left) illustrates the representation. A word, for example *catch*, has one vector describing the meaning of the word itself, the *lexical vector* $\vec{\text{catch}}$. It is a vector for the word in isolation, as is usual for prototype-based models. In addition, the representation for *catch* contains further vectors describing the *selectional preferences* for each argument position. The obj preference vector of *catch* is computed from the lexical vectors of all words that have been observed as direct objects of *catch* in some syntactically parsed corpus. In the example in Figure 2, we have observed the direct objects *cold, baseball,* and *drift.* In the simplest case, the obj preference vector of *catch* is then computed as the (weighted) sum of the three vectors $\vec{\text{cold}}$, $\vec{\text{baseball}}$ and $\vec{\text{drift}}$. Likewise, *ball* is represented by one vector for *ball* itself, one for *ball*'s preferences for its modifiers (mod), one vector for the verbs of which it is a subject ($subj^{-1}$), and one for the verbs of which is an object (obj^{-1}).

The vector for *catch* in a given context, say in the context *catch ball,* is then computed as illustrated on the right side of Figure 2: The lexical vector $\vec{\text{catch}}$ is combined with the obj^{-1} vector of *ball,* modifying the vector $\vec{\text{catch}}$ in the direction of verbs that typically take *ball* as an object. For the vector combination, any of the usual operations can be used: addition, component-wise multiplication, or minimum. Likewise, the lexical vector $\vec{\text{ball}}$ is combined with the obj preference vector of *catch* to compute the meaning of *ball* in the context *catch ball.*

The standard evaluation for vector models of meaning in context is to predict paraphrase appropriateness. Paraphrases always apply to a word meaning, not a word. For example, *contract* is an appropriate paraphrase for *catch* in the context *John caught the flu,* but it is not an appropriate paraphrase in the context *John caught a butterfly.* A vector space model can predict paraphrase appropriateness as the similarity (measured, for example, using Cosine) of the context-specific vector of *catch* with the lexical vector of *contract*: The more similar the vectors, the higher the predicted appropriateness of the paraphrase. We evaluated SVS on two datasets. The first is a tightly controlled psycholinguistic dataset of subject/verb pairs with paraphrases for the verbs only (Mitchell and Lapata, 2008). The other is the Lexical Substitution dataset, which has annotator-generated paraphrases for target words in a larger sentential context and which is thus closer to typical NLP application scenarios (McCarthy and Navigli, 2009). SVS showed comparable performance to the model by Mitchell and Lapata (2008) on the former dataset, and outperformed the Mitchell and Lapata model on the latter.

One obvious extension is to use all available syntactic context, instead of focusing on a single syntactic neighbor. We found no improvement on SVS in a straightforward extension to additional syntactic context items (Erk and Padó, 2009). However, Thater et al. (2009) did achieve better performance with a different model that used all syntactic context.

Taking larger context into account in an exemplar-based model. But even if we take the complete local syntactic context into account, we are missing some evidence, in particular non-local information. The word *ball* is interpreted differently in sentences (1a) and (1b) [1] even though its predicate *ran* has more or less the same meaning in both sentences. What is different is the subject of *ran*, *player* versus *debutante*, which is not a direct syntactic neighbor of the ambiguous word *ball*.

(1) (a) the player ran to the ball
(b) the debutante ran to the ball

Even though we are not using dictionary senses, the types of evidence that should be useful for computing occurrence-specific vectors should be the same as for traditional WSD; and one of the main type of features used there is bag-of-words context. In (Erk and Padó, 2010), we proposed an exemplar-based model of word meaning in context that relied on bag-of-words context information from the whole sentence, but did not use syntactic information. The model assumes that each target lemma is represented by a set of exemplars, where an exemplar is a sentence in which the target lemma occurs. Polysemy is then modeled by *activating* (selecting) relevant exemplars of a target lemma in a given occurrence s.[2] Both the exemplars and the occurrence s are modeled as vectors. We simply use first-order vectors that reflect the number of times each word occurs in a given sentence. The activated exemplars are then simply the ones whose vectors are most similar to the vector of s. The results that we achieved with the exemplar-based model on the Lexical Substitution dataset were considerably better than those achieved with any of the syntax-based approaches (Erk and Padó, 2008; Erk and Padó, 2009; Thater et al., 2009).

While prototype models compute a vector by first summing over all observed occurrences and then having to suppress dimensions that are not contextually appropriate, exemplar models only take contextually appropriate exemplars into account in the first place, which is conceptually simpler and thus more attractive. But there are still many open questions, in particular the best combination of bag-of-words context and syntactic context as evidence for computing occurrence-specific vector representations.

5 The role of dictionary senses

Word meaning models that rely only on individual word usages and their similarities are more flexible than dictionary-based models and make less assumptions. On the other hand, dictionaries offer not just sense lists but also a wealth of information that can be used for inferences. WordNet (Fellbaum, 1998) has relations between words and between synsets, most importantly synonymy and hyponymy. VerbNet (Kipper et al., 2000) specifies semantic properties of a predicate's arguments, as well as relations between the arguments.

In this section we discuss approaches for embedding dictionary senses in a distributional model in a way that supports hypotheses (A) and (B) (graded sense membership, and description of an occurrence through multiple senses) and that supports testing the applicability of dictionary-based inference rules.

Mapping dictionary senses to points in vector space. Dictionary senses can be mapped to points in vector space very straightforwardly if we have sense-annotated corpus data. In that case, we can compute a (prototype) vector for a sense from all corpus occurrences annotated with that sense. We used this simple model (Erk and McCarthy, 2009) to predict the graded sense applicability judgments from the WSsim dataset. (See Section 2 for more information on this dataset.) The predictions of the vector space model significantly correlate with annotator judgments. In comparison with an approach that uses the confidence levels of a standard WSD model as predictions, the vector space model shows higher recall but lower precision – for definitions of precision and recall that are adapted to the graded case.

[1]These two examples are due to Ray Mooney.

[2]Instead of the binary selection of each exemplar that this model uses, it would also be possible to assign each exemplar a weight, making it partially selected.

Another way of putting the findings is to say that the WSD confidence levels tend to under-estimate sense applicability, while the vector space model tends to over-estimate it.

Attachment sites for inference rules. As discussed above, vector space models for word meaning in context are typically evaluated on paraphrase applicability tasks (Mitchell and Lapata, 2008; Erk and Padó, 2008; Erk and Padó, 2009; Thater et al., 2009). They predict the applicability of a paraphrase like (2) based on the similarity between a context-specific vector for the lemma (here, *catch*) and a context-independent vector for the paraphrase. (in this case, *contract*).

$$X \text{ catch } Y \rightarrow X \text{ contract } Y \tag{2}$$

Another way of looking at this is to consider the inference rule (2) to be *attached* to a point in space, namely the vector for *contract*, and to trigger the inference rule for an occurrence of *catch* if it is close enough to the *attachment site*. If we know the WordNet sense of *contract* for which rule (2) holds – it happens to be sense 4 –, we can attach the rule to a vector for sense 4 of *contract*, rather than a vector computed from all occurrences of the lemma. Note that when we use dictionaries as a source for inference rules, for example by creating an inference rule like (2) for each two words that share a synset and for each direct hyponym/hypernym pair, we do know the WordNet sense to which each inference rule attaches.

Mapping dictionary senses to regions in vector space. In Erk (2009) we expand on the idea of tying inference rules to attachment sites by representing a word sense not as a point but as a *region* in vector space. The extent of the regions is estimated through the use of both positive exemplars (occurrences of the word sense in question), and negative exemplars (occurrences of other words). The computational models we use are inspired by cognitive models of concept representation that represent concepts as regions (Smith et al., 1988; Hampton, 1991), in particular adopting Shepard's law (Shepard, 1987), which states that perceived similarity to an exemplar decreases *exponentially* with distance from its vector.

In the longer term, the goal for the association of inference rules with attachment sites is to obtain a principled framework for reasoning with partially applicable inference rules in vector space.

6 Conclusion and outlook

In this paper, we have argued that it may be time to consider alternative computational models of word meaning, given that word sense disambiguation, after all this time, is still a tough problem for humans as well as machines. We have followed three hypotheses. The first two involve dictionary senses, suggesting that (A) senses may best be viewed as applying to a certain degree, rather than in a binary fashion, and (B) that it may make sense to describe an occurrence through multiple senses as a default rather than an exception. The third hypothesis then departs from dictionary senses, suggesting (C) focusing on individual word usages and their similarities instead. We have argued that distributional models are a good match for word meaning models following hypotheses (A)-(C): They can represent individual word usages as points in vector space, and they can also represent dictionary senses in a way that allows for graded membership and overlapping senses, and we have discussed some existing models, both prototype-based and exemplar-based.

One big question is, of course, about the usability of these alternative models of word meaning in NLP applications. Will they do better than dictionary-based models? The current evaluations, testing paraphrase applicability in context, are a step in the right direction, but more task-oriented evaluation schemes have to follow.

We have argued that it makes sense to look to cognitive models of mental concept representation. They are often based on feature vectors, and there are many interesting ideas in these models that have not yet been used (much) in computational models of word meaning. One of the most exciting ones, perhaps, is that cognitive models often have interpretable dimensions. While dimensions of distributional models are usually not individually interpretable, there are some first models (Almuhareb and Poesio, 2005; Baroni et al., 2010) that use patterns to extract meaningful dimensions from corpus data. This offers many new perspectives: For which tasks can we improve performance by selecting dimensions that are meaningful specifically for that task (as in Mitchell et al. (2008))? Can interpretable dimensions be used for inferences? And, when we are computing vector space representations for word meaning *in context*, is it possible to select meaningful dimensions that are appropriate for a given context?

Acknowledgements. This work was supported in part by National Science Foundation grant IIS-0845925, and by a Morris Memorial Grant from the New York Community Trust.

References

A. Almuhareb and M. Poesio. 2005. Finding concept attributes in the web. In *Proceedings of the Corpus Linguistics Conference*, Birmingham.

M. Sadrzadeh B. Coecke and S. Clark. 2010. Mathematical foundations for a compositional distributed model of meaning. *Lambek Festschrift, Linguistic Analysis*, 36.

M. Baroni, B. Murphy, E. Barbu, and M. Poesio. 2010. Strudel: A corpus-based semantic model based on properties and types. *Cognitive Science*, 34(2):222–254.

S. W. Brown. 2008. Choosing sense distinctions for WSD: Psycholinguistic evidence. In *Proceedings of ACL/HLT*, Columbus, OH.

J. Chen and M. Palmer. 2009. Improving English verb sense disambiguation performance with linguistically motivated features and clear sense distinction boundaries. *Journal of Language Resources and Evaluation, Special Issue on SemEval-2007*, 43:181–208.

L. Coleman and P. Kay. 1981. The English word "lie". *Linguistics*, 57.

D. A. Cruse. 1986. *Lexical Semantics*. Cambridge University Press.

S. Deerwester, S. T. Dumais, T. K. Landauer, G. W. Furnaas, and R. A. Harshman. 1990. Indexing by latent semantic analysis. *Journal of the Society for Information Science*, 41(6):391–407.

P. Edmonds and S. Cotton, editors. 2001. *Proceedings of the SensEval-2 Workshop*, Toulouse, France. ACL. See `http://www.sle.sharp.co.uk/senseval`.

K. Erk and D. McCarthy. 2009. Graded word sense assignment. In *Proceedings of EMNLP*, Singapore.

K. Erk and S. Padó. 2008. A structured vector space model for word meaning in context. In *Proceedings of EMNLP*, Honolulu, HI.

K. Erk and S. Padó. 2009. Paraphrase assessment in structured vector space: Exploring parameters and datasets. In *Proceedings of the EACL Workshop on Geometrical Methods for Natural Language Semantics (GEMS)*.

K. Erk and S. Padó. 2010. Exemplar-based models for word meaning in context. In *Proceedings of the ACL*, Uppsala.

K. Erk, D. McCarthy, and N. Gaylord. 2009. Investigations on word senses and word usages. In *Proceedings of ACL*, Singapore.

Katrin Erk. 2009. Representing words as regions in vector space. In *Proceedings of CoNLL*.

C. Fellbaum, editor. 1998. *WordNet: An electronic lexical database*. MIT Press, Cambridge, MA.

P. Gärdenfors. 2004. *Conceptual spaces*. MIT press, Cambridge, MA.

J. A. Hampton. 1979. Polymorphous concepts in semantic memory. *Journal of Verbal Learning and Verbal Behavior*, 18:441–461.

J. A. Hampton. 1991. The combination of prototype concepts. In P. Schwanenflugel, editor, *The psychology of word meanings*. Lawrence Erlbaum Associates.

J. A. Hampton. 2007. Typicality, graded membership, and vagueness. *Cognitive Science*, 31:355–384.

P. Hanks. 2000. Do word meanings exist? *Computers and the Humanities*, 34(1-2):205–215(11).

E. H. Hovy, M. Marcus, M. Palmer, S. Pradhan, L. Ramshaw, and R. Weischedel. 2006. OntoNotes: The 90% solution. In *Proceedings of HLT-NAACL*, pages 57–60, New York.

A. Kilgarriff and J. Rosenzweig. 2000. Framework and results for English Senseval. *Computers and the Humanities*, 34(1-2):15–48.

A. Kilgarriff. 1997. I don't believe in word senses. *Computers and the Humanities*, 31(2):91–113.

W. Kintsch. 2001. Predication. *Cognitive Science*, 25:173–202.

W. Kintsch. 2007. Meaning in context. In T.K. Landauer, D. McNamara, S. Dennis, and W. Kintsch, editors, *Handbook of Latent Semantic Analysis*, pages 89–105. Erlbaum, Mahwah, NJ.

K. Kipper, H.T. Dang, and M. Palmer. 2000. Class-based construction of a verb lexicon. In *Proceedings of AAAI/IAAI*.

D.E. Klein and G.L. Murphy. 2001. The representation of polysemous words. *Journal of Memory and Language*, 45:259–282.

G. Lakoff. 1987. *Women, fire, and dangerous things*. The University of Chicago Press.

T. Landauer and S. Dumais. 1997. A solution to Platos problem: the latent semantic analysis theory of acquisition, induction, and representation of knowledge. *Psychological Review*, 104(2):211–240.

S. Landes, C. Leacock, and R. Tengi. 1998. Building semantic concordances. In C. Fellbaum, editor, *WordNet: An Electronic Lexical Database*. The MIT Press, Cambridge, MA.

W. Lowe and S. McDonald. 2000. The direct route: Mediated priming in semantic space. In *Proceedings of the Cognitive Science Society*, pages 675–680.

K. Lund and C. Burgess. 1996. Producing high-dimensional semantic spaces from lexical co-occurrence. *Behavior Research Methods, Instruments, and Computers*, 28:203—208.

C. D. Manning, P. Raghavan, and H. Schütze. 2008. *Introduction to Information Retrieval*. Cambridge University Press.

D. McCarthy and R. Navigli. 2009. The English lexical substitution task. *Language Resources and Evaluation*, 43(2):139–159. Special Issue on Computational Semantic Analysis of Language: SemEval-2007 and Beyond.

D. McCarthy, R. Koeling, J. Weeds, and J. Carroll. 2004. Finding predominant senses in untagged text. In *Proceedings of ACL*, Barcelona.

M. McCloskey and S. Glucksberg. 1978. Natural categories: Well defined or fuzzy sets? *Memory & Cognition*, 6:462–472.

S. McDonald and M. Ramscar. 2001. Testing the distributional hypothesis: The influence of context on judgements of semantic similarity. In *Proceedings of the Cognitive Science Society*, pages 611–616.

K. McRae, G. S. Cree, M. S. Seidenberg, and C. McNorgan. 2005. Semantic feature production norms for a large set of living and nonliving things. *Behavior Research Methods*, 37(4):547–559.

D. L. Medin and M. M. Schaffer. 1978. Context theory of classification learning. *Psychological Review*, 85:207–238.

R. Mihalcea, T. Chklovski, and A. Kilgariff. 2004. The Senseval-3 English lexical sample task. In *Proceedings of SensEval-3*, Barcelona.

J. Mitchell and M. Lapata. 2008. Vector-based models of semantic composition. In *Proceedings of ACL*, Columbus, OH.

T. Mitchell, S. Shinkareva, A. Carlson, K. Chang, V.Malave, R. Mason, and M. Just. 2008. Predicting human brain activity associated with the meanings of nouns. *Science*, 320(5880):1191–1195.

G. L. Murphy. 1991. Meaning and concepts. In P. Schwanenflugel, editor, *The psychology of word meanings*. Lawrence Erlbaum Associates.

G. L. Murphy. 2002. *The Big Book of Concepts*. MIT Press.

R. M. Nosofsky and T. J. Palmeri. 1997. An exemplar-based random walk model of speeded classification. *Psychological Review*, 104(2):266–300.

R. M. Nosofsky. 1992. Exemplars, prototypes, and similarity rules. In A. Healy, S. Kosslyn, and R. Shiffrin, editors, *From learning theory to connectionist theory: essays in honor of W.K. Estes*, volume 1, pages 149–168. Erlbaum, Hillsdale, NJ.

S. Padó and M. Lapata. 2007. Dependency-based construction of semantic space models. *Computational Linguistics*, 33(2):161–199.

M. Palmer, H. Trang Dang, and C. Fellbaum. 2007. Making fine-grained and coarse-grained sense distinctions, both manually and automatically. *Natural Language Engineering*, 13:137–163.

P. Pantel and D. Lin. 2002. Discovering word senses from text. In *Proceedings of KDD*, Edmonton, Canada.

R. Passonneau, A. Salleb-Aouissi, V. Bhardwaj, and N. Ide. 2010. Word sense annotation of polysemous words by multiple annotators. In *Proceedings of LREC-7*, Valleta, Malta.

S. Pradhan, E. Loper, D. Dligach, and M. Palmer. 2007. Semeval-2007 task 17: English lexical sample, SRL and all words. In *Proceedings of SemEval¡*, Prague, Czech Republic.

L. Pylkkanen, R. Llinas, and G.L. Murphy. 2006. The representation of polysemy: MEG evidence. *Journal of Cognitive Neuroscience*, 18:97–109.

J. Reisinger and R.J. Mooney. 2010. Multi-prototype vector-space models of word meaning. In *Proceeding of NAACL*.

E. Rosch and C. B. Mervis. 1975. Family resemblance: Studies in the internal structure of categories. *Cognitive Psychology*, 7:573–605.

E. Rosch. 1975. Cognitive representations of semantic categories. *Journal of Experimental Psychology: General*, 104:192–233.

M. Sahlgren and J. Karlgren. 2005. Automatic bilingual lexicon acquisition using random indexing of parallel corpora. *Journal of Natural Language Engineering, Special Issue on Parallel Texts*, 11(3).

H. Schütze. 1998. Automatic word sense discrimination. *Computational Linguistics*, 24(1).

R. Shepard. 1987. Towards a universal law of generalization for psychological science. *Science*, 237(4820):1317–1323.

E. E. Smith and D. L. Medin. 1981. *Categories and Concepts*. Harvard University Press, Cambridge, MA.

E. E. Smith, D. Osherson, L. J. Rips, and M. Keane. 1988. Combining prototypes: A selective modification model. *Cognitive Science*, 12(4):485–527.

P. Smolensky. 1990. Tensor product variable binding and the representation of symbolic structures in connectionist systems. *Artificial Intelligence*, 46:159–216.

B. Snyder and M. Palmer. 2004. The English all-words task. In *3rd International Workshop on Semantic Evaluations (SensEval-3) at ACL-2004*, Barcelona, Spain.

J. Taylor. 1989. *Linguistic Categorization: Prototypes in Linguistic Theory*. Oxford Textbooks in Linguistics.

S. Thater, G. Dinu, and M. Pinkal. 2009. Ranking paraphrases in context. In *Proceedings of the ACL Workshop on Applied Textual Inference*, Singapore.

D. H. Tuggy. 1993. Ambiguity, polysemy and vagueness. *Cognitive linguistics*, 4(2):273–290.

G. Vigliocco, D. P. Vinson, W. Lewis, and M. F. Garrett. 2004. Representing the meanings of object and action words: The featural and unitary semantic space hypothesis. *Cognitive Psychology*, 48:422–488.

W. Weaver. 1949. Translation. In W.N. Locke and A.D. Booth, editors, *Machine Translation of Languages: Fourteen Essays*. MIT Press, Cambridge, MA.

Relatedness Curves for Acquiring Paraphrases

Georgiana Dinu
Saarland University
Saarbruecken, Germany
dinu@coli.uni-sb.de

Grzegorz Chrupała
Saarland University
Saarbruecken, Germany
gchrupala@lsv.uni-saarland.de

Abstract

In this paper we investigate methods for computing similarity of two phrases based on their relatedness scores across *all* ranks k in a SVD approximation of a phrase/term co-occurrence matrix. We confirm the major observations made in previous work and our preliminary experiments indicate that these methods can lead to reliable similarity scores which in turn can be used for the task of paraphrasing.

1 Introduction

Distributional methods for word similarity use large amounts of text to acquire similarity judgments based solely on co-occurrence statistics. Typically each word is assigned a representation as a point in a high dimensional space, where the dimensions represent contextual features; following this, vector similarity measures are used to judge the meaning relatedness of words. One way to make these computations more reliable is to use Singular Value Decomposition (SVD) in order to obtain a lower rank approximation of an original co-occurrence matrix.

SVD is a matrix factorization method which has applications in a large number of fields such as signal processing or statistics. In natural language processing methods such as Latent Semantic Analysis (LSA) (Deerwester et al., 1990) use SVD to obtain a factorization of a (typically) word/document co-occurrence matrix. The underlying idea in these models is that the dimensionality reduction will produce meaningful dimensions which represent concepts rather than just terms, rendering similarity measures on these vectors more accurate. Over the years, it has been shown that these methods can closely match human similarity judgments and that they can be used in various applications such as information retrieval, document classification, essay grading etc. However it has been noted that the success of these methods is drastically determined by the choice of dimension k to which the original space is reduced.

(Bast and Majumdar, 2005) investigates exactly this aspect and proves that no fixed choice of dimension is appropriate. The authors show that two terms can be reliably compared only by investigating the curve of their relatedness scores over all dimensions k. The authors use a term/document matrix and analyze relatedness curves for inducing a hard related/not-related decision and show that their algorithms significantly improve over previous methods for information retrieval.

In this paper we investigate: 1) how the findings of (Bast and Majumdar, 2005) carry over to acquiring paraphrases using SVD on a *phrase/term* co-occurrence matrix and 2) if reliable similarity scores can be obtained from the analysis of relatedness curves.

2 Background

2.1 Singular Value Decomposition

Models such as LSA use Singular Value Decomposition, in order to obtain term representations over a space of *concepts*.

Given a co-occurrence matrix X of size (t, d), we can compute the singular value decomposition: $U\Sigma V^T$ of rank r. Matrices U and V^T of sizes (t, r) and (r, d) are the left and right singular vectors; Σ is the (r, r) diagonal matrix of singular values (ordered in descending order)[1]. Similarity between terms i and j is computed as the scalar product between the two vectors associated to the words in the U matrix:

$$sim(u_i, u_j) = \Sigma_{l=1}^{k} u_{il} u_{jl}$$

[1] Any approximation of rank $k < r$ can simply be obtained from an approximation or rank r by deleting rows and columns.

Proceedings of the 2010 Workshop on GEometrical Models of Natural Language Semantics, ACL 2010, pages 27–32,
Uppsala, Sweden, 16 July 2010.

2.2 Relatedness curves

Finding the optimal dimensionality k has proven to be an extremely important and not trivial step. (Bast and Majumdar, 2005) show that no single cut dimension is appropriate to compute the similarity of two terms but this should be deduced from the curve of similarity scores over all dimensions k. The curve of relatedness for two terms u_i and u_j is given by their scalar product across all dimensions k, k smaller than a rank r:

$$k \rightarrow \Sigma_{l=1}^{k} u_{il} u_{jl},\ for\ k = 1, ..., r$$

They show that a smooth curve indicates closely related terms, while a curve exhibiting many direction changes indicates unrelated terms; the actual values of the similarity scores are often misleading, which explains why a good cut dimension k is so difficult to find.

2.3 Vector space representation of phrases

We choose to apply this to acquiring paraphrases (or inference rules, i.e. entailments which hold in just one direction) in the sense of DIRT (Lin and Pantel, 2001).

In the DIRT algorithm a phrase is a noun-ending path in a dependency graph and the goal is to acquire inference rules such as *(X solve Y, X find solution to Y)*. We will call dependency paths *patterns*. The input data consists of large amounts of parsed text, from which patterns together with X-filler and Y-filler frequency counts are extracted.

In this setting, a pattern receives two vector representation, one in a **X**-filler space and one in the **Y**-filler space. In order to compute the similarity between two patterns, these are compared in the X space and in the Y space, and the two resulting scores are multiplied. (The DIRT algorithm uses Lin measure for computing similarity, which is given in Section 4). Obtaining these vectors from the frequency counts is straightforward and it is exemplified in Table 1 which shows a fragment of a Y-filler DIRT-like vector space.

	..	*case*	*problem*	..
(*X solve Y*, **Y**)	..	6.1	4.4	..
(*X settle Y*, **Y**)	..	5.2	5.9	..

Table 1: DIRT-like vector representation in the **Y**-filler space. The values represent mutual information.

3 Relatedness curves for acquiring paraphrases

3.1 Setup

We parsed the XIE fragment of GigaWord (approx. 100 mil. tokens) with Stanford dependency parser. From this we built a pattern/word matrix of size (85000, 3000) containing co-occurrence data of the most frequent patterns with the most frequent words[2]. We perform SVD factorization on this matrix of rank $k = 800$. For each pair of patterns, we can associate two relatedness curves: a X curve and Y curve given by the scalar products of their vectors in the U matrix, across dimensions $k : 1, ..., 800$.

3.2 Evaluating smoothness of the relatedness curves

In Figure 1 we plotted the X and Y curves of comparing the pattern $X \xleftarrow{subj} win \xrightarrow{dobj} Y$ with itself.

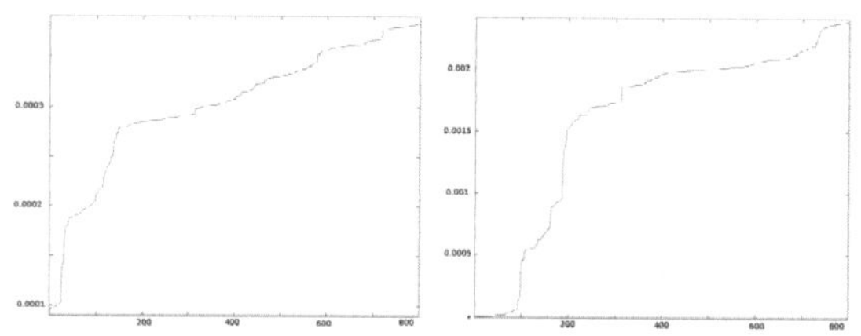

Figure 1: **X-filler** and **Y-filler** relatedness curves for the identity pair $(X \xleftarrow{subj} win \xrightarrow{dobj} Y, X \xleftarrow{subj} win \xrightarrow{dobj} Y)$

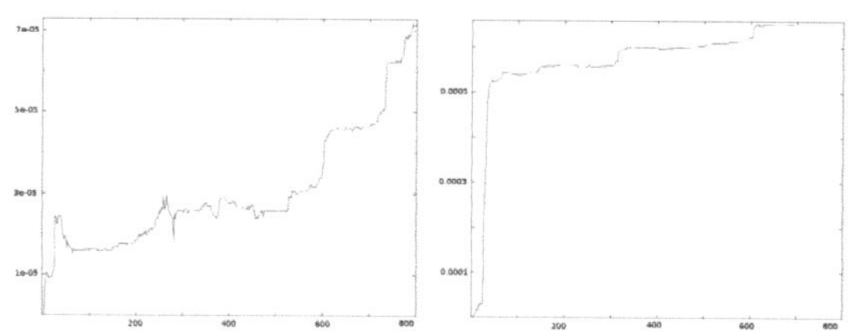

Figure 2: **X-filler** and **Y-filler** relatedness curves for $(X \xleftarrow{subj} leader \xrightarrow{prp} of \xrightarrow{pobj} Y, X \xleftarrow{pobj} by \xleftarrow{prp} lead \xrightarrow{subj} Y)$

Normally, the X and Y curves for the identical pair are monotonically increasing. However what can be noticed is that the actual values of these functions differ by one order of magnitude in the X and in the Y curves of identical patterns, showing that in themselves they are not a good indica-

[2]Even if conceptually we have two semantic spaces (given by X-fillers and Y-fillers), in reality we can work with a single matrix, containing for each pattern also its reverse, both represented solely in a X-filler space

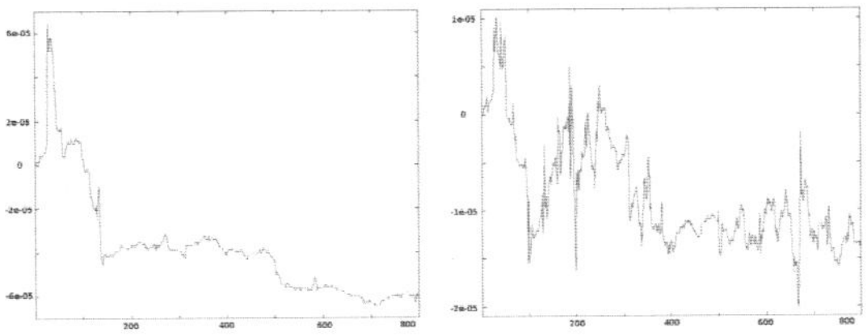

Figure 3: **X-filler** and **Y-filler** relatedness curves for $(X \xleftarrow{subj} win \xrightarrow{dobj} Y, X \xleftarrow{subj} murder \xrightarrow{dobj} Y)$

tor of similarity. In Figure 2 we investigate a pair of closely related patterns: $(X \xleftarrow{subj} leader \xrightarrow{prp} of \xrightarrow{pobj} Y, X \xleftarrow{pobj} by \xleftarrow{prp} lead \xrightarrow{subj} Y)$. It can be noticed that while still not comparable to those of the identical pair, these curves are much smoother than the ones associated to the pair of unrelated patterns in Figure 3[3].

However, unlike in the information retrieval scenario in (Bast and Majumdar, 2005), for which a hard related/not-related assignment works best, for acquiring paraphrases we need to quantify the smoothness of the curves. We describe two functions for evaluating curve smoothness which we will use to compute scores in X-filler and Y-filler semantic spaces.

Smooth function 1 This function simply computes the number of changes in the direction of the curve, as the percentage of times the scalar product increases or remains equal from step l to step $l+1$:

$$CurveS1(u_i, u_j) = \frac{\Sigma_{u_{il}u_{jl} \geq 0} 1}{k},\ l = 1, ..., k$$

An increasing curve will be assigned the maximal value 1, while for a curve that is monotonically decreasing the score will be 0.

Smooth function 2 (Bast and Majumdar, 2005) The second smooth function is given by:

$$CurveS2(u_i, u_j) = \frac{max - min}{\Sigma_{l=1}^{k} abs(u_{il}u_{jl})}$$

where max and min are the largest and smallest values in the curves. A curve which is always increasing or always decreasing will get a score of 1. Unlike the previous method this function is sensitive to the absolute values in the drops of a curve. A curve with large drops, irrelevant of their cardinality, will be penalized by being assigned a low score.

[3]The drop out dimension discussed in (Bast and Majumdar, 2005) Section 3, does not seem to exist for our data. This is to be expected since this result stems from a definition of perfectly related terms which is adapted to the particularities of term/document matrices, and not of term/term matrices.

4 Experimental results

In order to compute the similarity score between two phrases, we follow (Lin and Pantel, 2001) and compute two similarity scores, corresponding to the X-fillers and Y-fillers, and multiply them. Given a similarity function, any pattern encountered in the corpus can be paraphrased by returning its most similar patterns.

We implement five similarity functions on the data we have described in the previous section. The first one is the **DIRT** algorithm and it is the only method using the original co-occurrence matrix in which raw counts are replaced by point-wise mutual information scores.

DIRT method The similarity function for two vectors p_i and p_j is:

$$\text{sim}_{\text{Lin}}(p_i, p_j) = \frac{\sum_{l \in I(p_i) \cap I(p_j)} (p_{il} + p_{jl})}{\sum_{l \in I(p_i)} p_{il} + \sum_{l \in I(p_j)} p_{jl}}$$

where values in p_i and p_j are point-wise mutual information, and $I(\cdot)$ gives the indices of non-negative values in a vector.

Methods on SVD factorization All these methods perform computations the (85000, 800) U matrix in the SVD factorization. On this we implement two methods which do an arbitrary dimension cut of $k = 600$: 1) **SP-600** (scalar product) and 2) **COS-600** (cosine similarity). The other two algorithms: **CurveS1** and **CurveS2** use the two curve smoothness functions in Section 3.2; the curves plot the scalar product corresponding to the two patterns, from dimension 1 to 800.

Data In these preliminary experiments we limit ourselves to paraphrasing a set of patterns extracted from a subset of the TREC02-TREC06 question answering tracks. From these questions we extracted and paraphrased the most frequently occurring 20 patterns. Since judging the correctness of these paraphrases "out-of-context" is rather difficult we limit ourselves to giving examples and analyzing errors made on this data; important observations can be clearly made this way, however in future work we plan to build a proper evaluation setting (e.g. task-based or instance-based in the sense of (Szpektor et al., 2007)) for a more detailed analysis of the performance on the methods discussed.

4.1 Results

We list the paraphrases obtained with the different methods for the pattern $X \xleftarrow{subj} show \xrightarrow{dobj} Y$. This pattern has been chosen out of the total set due to its medium difficulty in terms of paraphrasing; some of the patterns in our list are relatively accurately paraphrased by all methods, such as *win*, while others such as *marry* are almost impossible to paraphrase, for all methods. In Table 2 we list the top 10 expansions returned by the four methods using the SVD factorization. In bold we mark correct patterns, which we consider to be patterns for which there is a context in which the entailment holds in at least one direction.

As it is clearly reflected in this example the SP-600 is much worse than any of the curve analysis methods; however using cosine as similarity measure at the same arbitrarily chosen dimension (COS-600) brings major improvements.

The two curve smoothness methods exhibit a systematic difference between them. In this example, and also across all 20 instances we have considered, CurveS1 ranks as most similar, a large variety of patterns with the same lexical root (in which, of course, syntax is often incorrect). Only following this we can find patterns expressing lexical variations; these again will be present in many syntactic variations. This sets CurveS1 apart from both CurveS2 and from COS-600 methods. These latter two methods, although conceptually different seem to exhibit surprisingly similar behavior. The behavior of CurveS1 smoothing method is difficult to judge without a proper evaluation; it can be the case that the errors (mostly in syntactic relations) are indeed errors of the algorithm or that the parser introduces them already in our input data.

Table 3 shows the top 10 paraphrases returned by the DIRT algorithm. The DIRT paraphrases are rather accurate, however it is interesting to observe that DIRT and SVD methods can extract different paraphrases. Table 4 gives examples of correct paraphrases which are identified by DIRT but not CurveS2 and the other way around. This seems to indicate that these algorithms do capture different aspects of the data and can be combined for better results. An important aspect here is the fact that obtaining highly accurate paraphrases at the cost of losing coverage is not particularly difficult[4] however not very useful. Previous work such as (Dinu and Wang, 2009) has shown that for these resources, the coverage is a rather important aspect, since they have to capture the great variety of ways in which a meaning can be expressed in different contexts.

DIRT
$\xleftarrow{subj}$ **reflect** $\xrightarrow{dobj}$
$\xleftarrow{subj}$ **indicate** $\xrightarrow{dobj}$
$\xleftarrow{subj}$ **demonstrate** $\xrightarrow{dobj}$
$\xleftarrow{pobj}$ **in** $\xleftarrow{prp}$ **show** $\xrightarrow{dobj}$
$\xleftarrow{pobj} to \xleftarrow{prp} show \xrightarrow{dobj}$
$\xleftarrow{subj}$ **represent** $\xrightarrow{dobj}$
$\xleftarrow{subj}$ **show** $\xrightarrow{prp}$ **in** $\xrightarrow{pobj}$
$\xleftarrow{subj}$ **display** $\xrightarrow{dobj}$
$\xleftarrow{subj} bring \xrightarrow{dobj}$
$\xleftarrow{pobj}$ **with** $\xleftarrow{prp}$ **show** $\xrightarrow{dobj}$

Table 3: Top 10 paraphrases for $X \xleftarrow{subj} show \xrightarrow{dobj} Y$

CurveS2	DIRT
$\xleftarrow{subj}$ **show** $\xrightarrow{dobj}$	
$\xleftarrow{pobj} in \xleftarrow{prp} indicate \xrightarrow{dobj}$	$\xleftarrow{subj} display \xrightarrow{dobj}$
$\xleftarrow{pobj} in \xleftarrow{prp} reflect \xrightarrow{dobj}$	$\xleftarrow{subj} confirm \xrightarrow{dobj}$
$\xleftarrow{dobj} interpret \xrightarrow{prp} as \xrightarrow{pobj}$	$\xleftarrow{subj} point \xrightarrow{prp} to \xrightarrow{pobj}$
$\xleftarrow{subj}$ **win** $\xrightarrow{dobj}$	
$\xleftarrow{subj} vie \xrightarrow{prp} for \xrightarrow{pobj}$	$\xleftarrow{pos} victory \xrightarrow{prp} in \xrightarrow{pobj}$
$\xleftarrow{subj} compete \xrightarrow{prp} for \xrightarrow{pobj}$	$\xleftarrow{subj} win \xrightarrow{dobj} title \xrightarrow{nn}$
$\xleftarrow{subj} secure \xrightarrow{dobj}$	$\xrightarrow{appos} winner \xrightarrow{nn}$
$\xleftarrow{subj}$ **enter** $\xrightarrow{dobj}$	
$\xleftarrow{subj} march \xrightarrow{prp} into \xrightarrow{pobj}$	$\xleftarrow{subj} start \xrightarrow{prp} in \xrightarrow{pobj}$
$\xleftarrow{subj} advance \xrightarrow{prp} into \xrightarrow{pobj}$	$\xleftarrow{subj} play \xrightarrow{prp} in \xrightarrow{pobj}$
$\xleftarrow{pos} entry \xrightarrow{prp} to \xrightarrow{pobj}$	$\xleftarrow{subj} join \xrightarrow{prp} in \xrightarrow{pobj}$

Table 4: Example of paraphrases (i.e. ranked in the top 30) identified by one method and not the other

4.2 Discussion

In this section we attempt to get more insight into the way the relatedness curves relate to the intuitive notion of similarity, by examining curves of incorrect paraphrases extracted by our methods.

The first error we consider, is the pattern $X \xleftarrow{pos} confidence \xleftarrow{pobj} of \xleftarrow{prp} Y$ which is judged as being very similar to *show* by SP-600, COS-600 as well as CurveS2. Figure 4 shows the relatedness curves. As it can be noticed, both the X and Y similarities grow dramatically around dimension

[4]High precision can be very easily achieved simply by intersecting the sets of paraphrases returned by two or more of the methods implemented

SP-600	COS-600	CurveS1	CurveS2
$\xleftarrow{pos} confidence \xleftarrow{pobj} of \xleftarrow{prp}$	$\xleftarrow{\mathbf{subj}} \mathbf{indicate} \xrightarrow{\mathbf{dobj}}$	$\xleftarrow{\mathbf{subj}} \mathbf{show} \xrightarrow{\mathbf{prp}} \mathbf{in} \xrightarrow{\mathbf{pobj}}$	$\xleftarrow{\mathbf{subj}} \mathbf{indicate} \xrightarrow{\mathbf{dobj}}$
$\xleftarrow{subj} boost \xrightarrow{dobj} rate \xrightarrow{nn}$	$\xleftarrow{\mathbf{subj}} \mathbf{show} \xrightarrow{\mathbf{prp}} \mathbf{of} \xrightarrow{\mathbf{pobj}}$	$\xleftarrow{\mathbf{subj}} \mathbf{indicate} \xrightarrow{\mathbf{dobj}}$	$\xleftarrow{\mathbf{subj}} \mathbf{reflect} \xrightarrow{\mathbf{dobj}}$
$\xleftarrow{\mathbf{subj}} \mathbf{show} \xrightarrow{\mathbf{prp}} \mathbf{of} \xrightarrow{\mathbf{pobj}}$	$\xleftarrow{\mathbf{subj}} \mathbf{represent} \xrightarrow{\mathbf{dobj}}$	$\xleftarrow{subj} show \xrightarrow{prp} with \xrightarrow{pobj}$	$\xleftarrow{\mathbf{subj}} \mathbf{represent} \xrightarrow{\mathbf{dobj}}$
$\xrightarrow{prp} to \xrightarrow{pobj} percent \xrightarrow{nn}$	$\xleftarrow{\mathbf{pobj}} \mathbf{by} \xleftarrow{\mathbf{prp}} \mathbf{show} \xleftarrow{\mathbf{partmod}}$	$\xleftarrow{\mathbf{pobj}} \mathbf{with} \xleftarrow{\mathbf{prp}} \mathbf{show} \xrightarrow{\mathbf{dobj}}$	$\xleftarrow{subj} bring \xrightarrow{dobj} rate \xrightarrow{nn}$
$\xleftarrow{subj} total \xrightarrow{dobj} yuan \xrightarrow{appos}$	$\xleftarrow{\mathbf{pobj}} \mathbf{in} \xleftarrow{\mathbf{prp}} \mathbf{reflect} \xrightarrow{\mathbf{dobj}}$	$\xleftarrow{subj} show \xrightarrow{tmod}$	$\xleftarrow{\mathbf{subj}} \mathbf{show} \xrightarrow{\mathbf{prp}} \mathbf{of} \xrightarrow{\mathbf{pobj}}$
$\xleftarrow{subj} hit \xrightarrow{dobj} dollar \xrightarrow{appos}$	$\xleftarrow{pos} confidence \xleftarrow{pobj} of \xleftarrow{prp}$	$\xleftarrow{subj} show \xrightarrow{prp} despite \xrightarrow{pobj}$	$\xleftarrow{\mathbf{dobj}} \mathbf{interpret} \xrightarrow{\mathbf{prp}} \mathbf{as} \xrightarrow{\mathbf{pobj}}$
$\xleftarrow{subj} reach \xrightarrow{dobj} dollar \xrightarrow{appos}$	$\xleftarrow{\mathbf{pobj}} \mathbf{by} \xleftarrow{\mathbf{prp}} \mathbf{reflect} \xrightarrow{\mathbf{dobj}}$	$\xleftarrow{pobj} during \xleftarrow{prp} show \xrightarrow{dobj}$	$\xleftarrow{pos} confidence \xleftarrow{pobj} of \xleftarrow{prp}$
$\xleftarrow{subj} slash \xrightarrow{dobj} rate \xrightarrow{nn}$	$\xleftarrow{\mathbf{pobj}} \mathbf{in} \xleftarrow{\mathbf{prp}} \mathbf{indicate} \xrightarrow{\mathbf{dobj}}$	$\xleftarrow{\mathbf{pobj}} \mathbf{in} \xleftarrow{\mathbf{prp}} \mathbf{show} \xrightarrow{\mathbf{dobj}}$	$\xleftarrow{\mathbf{subj}} \mathbf{show} \xrightarrow{\mathbf{dobj}} \mathbf{rate} \xrightarrow{\mathbf{nn}}$
$\xleftarrow{nn} confidence \xleftarrow{pobj} of \xleftarrow{prp}$	$\xleftarrow{\mathbf{subj}} \mathbf{reflect} \xrightarrow{\mathbf{dobj}}$	$\xleftarrow{\mathbf{pobj}} \mathbf{by} \xleftarrow{\mathbf{prp}} \mathbf{show} \xleftarrow{\mathbf{partmod}}$	$\xleftarrow{subj} put \xrightarrow{dobj} rate \xrightarrow{nn}$
$\xleftarrow{subj} raise \xrightarrow{dobj} rate \xrightarrow{nn}$	$\xleftarrow{subj} interpret \xrightarrow{prp} as \xrightarrow{pobj}$	$\xleftarrow{\mathbf{pobj}} \mathbf{on} \xleftarrow{\mathbf{prp}} \mathbf{show} \xrightarrow{\mathbf{dobj}}$	$\xleftarrow{\mathbf{pobj}} \mathbf{by} \xleftarrow{\mathbf{prp}} \mathbf{show} \xleftarrow{\mathbf{partmod}}$

Table 2: Top 10 paraphrases for $X \xleftarrow{subj} show \xrightarrow{dobj} Y$

500. Therefore the scalar product will be very high at cut point 600, leading to methods' SP-600 and COS-600 error. However the two curve methods are sensitive to the shape of the relatedness curves. Since CurveS2 is sensitive to actual drop values in these curves, this pair will still be ranked very similar. The curves do decrease by small amounts in *many* points which is why method CurveS1 does score these two patterns as very similar.

An interesting point to be made here is that, this pair is ranked similar by three methods out of four because of the dramatic increase in relatedness at around dimension 500. However, intuitively, such an increase should be more relevant at earlier dimensions, which correspond to the larger eigenvalues, and therefore to the most relevant concepts. Indeed, in the data we have analyzed, highly similar patterns exhibit large increases at earlier (first 100-200) dimensions, similarly to the examples given in Figure 1 and Figure 2. This leads us to a particular aspect that we would like to investigate in future work, which is to analyze the behavior of a relatedness curve in relation to relevance weights obtained from the eigenvalues of the matrix factorization.

In Figure 5 we plot a second error, the relatedness curves of *show* with $X \xleftarrow{subj} boost \xrightarrow{dobj} rate \xrightarrow{nn} Y$ which is as error made only by the SP-600 method. The similarity reflected in curve Y is relatively high (given by the large overlap of Y-filler $interest$), however we obtain a very high X similarity only due to the peak of the scalar product exactly around the cut dimension 600.

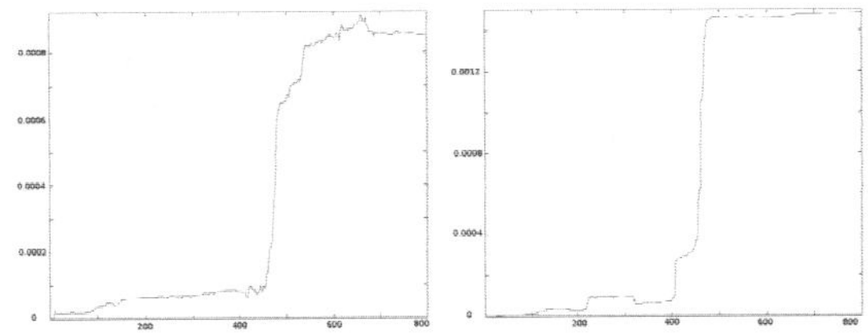

Figure 4: **X-filler** and **Y-filler** relatedness curves for $(X \xleftarrow{subj} show \xrightarrow{dobj} Y, X \xleftarrow{pos} confidence \xleftarrow{pobj} of \xleftarrow{prp} Y)$

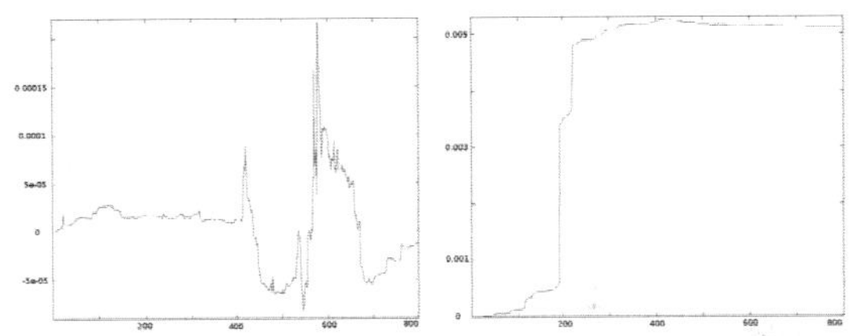

Figure 5: **X-filler** and **Y-filler** relatedness curves for $(X \xleftarrow{subj} show \xrightarrow{dobj} Y, X \xleftarrow{subj} boost \xrightarrow{dobj} rate \xrightarrow{nn} Y)$

5 Conclusion

In this paper we have investigated the relevance of judging similarity of two phrases across all ranks k in a SVD approximation of a phrase/term co-occurrence matrix. We confirm the major observations made in previous work and our preliminary experiments indicate that reliable similarity scores for paraphrasing can be obtained from the analysis of relatedness scores across all dimensions.

In the future we plan to 1) use the observations we have made in Section 4.2 to focus on identifying good curve-smoothness functions and 2) build an appropriate evaluation setting in order to be able to accurately judge the performance of the methods we propose.

Finally, in this paper we have investigated these aspects for the task of paraphrasing in a particular setting, however our findings can be applied to any vector space method for semantic similarity.

References

Scott C. Deerwester and Susan T. Dumais and Thomas K. Landauer and George W. Furnas and Richard A. Harshman 1990. *Indexing by Latent Semantic Analysis In JASIS.*

Bast, Holger and Majumdar, Debapriyo. 2005. Why spectral retrieval works. *SIGIR '05: Proceedings of the 28th annual international ACM SIGIR conference on Research and development in information retrieval.*

Dekang Lin and Patrick Pantel. 2001. DIRT - Discovery of Inference Rules from Text. *In Proceedings of the ACM SIGKDD Conference on Knowledge Discovery and Data Mining.*

Georgiana Dinu and Rui Wang. 2009. Inference rules and their application to recognizing textual entailment. *In Proceedings of the 12th Conference of the European Chapter of the ACL (EACL 2009).*

Idan Szpektor and Eyal Shnarch and Ido Dagan 2007. Instance-based Evaluation of Entailment Rule Acquisition. *In Proceedings of the 45th Annual Meeting of the Association for Computational Linguistics.*

A Regression Model of Adjective-Noun Compositionality in Distributional Semantics

Emiliano Guevara
Tekstlab, ILN, University of Oslo
Oslo, Norway
e.r.guevara@iln.uio.no

Abstract

In this paper we explore the computational modelling of compositionality in distributional models of semantics. In particular, we model the semantic composition of pairs of adjacent English Adjectives and Nouns from the *British National Corpus*. We build a vector-based semantic space from a lemmatised version of the BNC, where the most frequent A-N lemma pairs are treated as single tokens. We then extrapolate three different models of compositionality: a simple additive model, a pointwise-multiplicative model and a Partial Least Squares Regression (PLSR) model. We propose two evaluation methods for the implemented models. Our study leads to the conclusion that regression-based models of compositionality generally out-perform additive and multiplicative approaches, and also show a number of advantages that make them very promising for future research.

1 Introduction

Word-space vector models or distributional models of semantics (henceforth DSMs), are computational models that build contextual semantic representations for lexical items from corpus data. DSMs have been successfully used in the recent years for a number of different computational tasks involving semantic relations between words (e.g. synonym identification, computation of semantic similarity, modelling selectional preferences, etc., for a thorough discussion of the field, cf. Sahlgren, 2006). The theoretical foundation of DSMs is to be found in the "distributional hypothesis of meaning", attributed to Z. Harris, which maintains that meaning is susceptible to distributional analysis and, in particular, that differences in meaning between **words** or **morphemes** in a language correlate with differences in their distribution (Harris 1970, pp. 784–787).

While the vector-based representation of word meaning has been used for a long time in computational linguistics, the techniques that are currently used have not seen much development with regards to one of the main aspects of semantics in natural language: compositionality.

To be fair, the study of semantic compositionality in DSMs has seen a slight revival in the recent times, cf. Widdows (2008), Mitchell & Lapata (2008), Giesbrecht (2009), Baroni & Lenci (2009), who propose various DSM approaches to represent argument structure, subject-verb and verb-object co-selection. Current approaches to compositionality in DSMs are based on the application of a simple geometric operation on the basis of individual vectors (vector addition, pointwise-multiplication of corresponding dimensions, tensor product) which should in principle approximate the composition of any two given vectors.

On the contrary, since the the very nature of compositionality depends on the **semantic relation** being instantiated in a syntactic structure, we propose that the composition of vector representations must be modelled as a relation-specific phenomenon. In particular, we propose that the usual procedures from machine learning tasks must be implemented also in the search for semantic compositionality in DSM.

In this paper we present work in progress on the computational modelling of compositionality in a data-set of English Adjective-Noun pairs extracted from the BNC. We extrapolate three different models of compositionality: a simple additive model, a pointwise-multiplicative model and, finally, a multinomial multiple regression model by Partial Least Squares Regression (PLSR).

Proceedings of the 2010 Workshop on GEometrical Models of Natural Language Semantics, ACL 2010, pages 33–37,
Uppsala, Sweden, 16 July 2010.

2 Compositionality of meaning in DSMs

Previous work in the field has produced a small number of operations to represent the composition of vectorial representations of word meaning. In particular, given two independent vectors *v1* and *v2*, the semantically compositional result *v3* is modelled by:

- **vector addition**, the compositional meaning of *v3* consists of the sum of the independent vectors for the constituent words:
  $v1_i + v2_i = v3_i$
- **pointwise-multiplication** (Mitchell and Lapata 2008), each corresponding pair of components of *v1* and *v2* are multiplied to obtain the corresponding component of *v3*:
  $v1_i \times v2_i = v3_i$
- **tensor product**, $v1 \otimes v2 = v3$, where $v3$ is a matrix whose *ij*-th entry is equal to $v1_i v2_j$ (cf. Widdows 2008, who also proposes the related method of **convolution product**, both imported from the field of quantum mechanics)

In the DSM literature, the additive model has become a *de facto* standard approach to approximate the composed meaning of a group of words (or a document) as the **sum** of their vectors (which results in the centroid of the starting vectors). This has been successfully applied to document-based applications such as the computation of document similarity in information retrieval.

Mitchell & Lapata (2008) indicate that the various variations of the **pointwise-multiplication** model perform better than simple additive models in term similarity tasks (variations included combination with simple addition and adding weights to individual vector components). Widdows (2008) Obtain results indicating that both the **tensor product** and the **convolution product** perform better than the simple additive model.

For the sake of simplifying the implementation of evaluation methods, in this paper we will compare the first two approaches, vector addition and vector pointwise-multiplication, with regression modelling by partial least squares.

3 Partial least squares regression of compositionality

We assume that the composition of meaning in DSMs is a function mapping two or more independent vectors in a multidimensional space to a newly composed vector the same space and, further, we assume that semantic composition is dependent on the syntactic structure being instantiated in natural language.[1]

Assuming that each dimension in the starting vectors $v1$ and $v2$ is a candidate predictor, and that each dimension in the composed vector $v3$ is a dependent variable, vector-based semantic compositionality can be formulated as a problem of multivariate multiple regression. This is, in principle, a tractable problem that can be solved by standard machine learning techniques such as multilayer perceptrons or support vector machines.

However, given that sequences of words tend to be of very low frequency (and thus difficult to represent in a DSM), suitable data sets will inevitably suffer the curse of dimensionality: we will often have many more variables (dimensions) than observations.

Partial Least Squares Regression (PLSR) is a multivariate regression technique that has been designed specifically to tackle such situations with high dimensionality and limited data. PLSR is widely used in in unrelated fields such as spectroscopy, medical chemistry, brain-imaging and marketing (Mevik & Wehrens, 2007).

4 Materials and tools

We use a general-purpose vector space extracted from the British National Corpus. We used the *Infomap* software to collect co-occurrence statistics for lemmas within a rectangular 5L–5R window. The corpus was pre-processed to represent frequent Adjective-Noun lemma pairs as a single token (e.g. while in the original corpus the A-N phrase *nice house* consists in two separate lemmas (*nice* and *house*), in the processed corpus it appears as a single entry *nice_house*). The corpus was also processed by stop-word removal. We extracted a list of A-N candidate pairs with simple regex-based queries targeting adjacent sequences composed of [Det/Art–A–N] (e.g. *that little house*). We filtered the candidate list by frequency ($>$ 400) obtaining 1,380 different A-N pairs.

The vector space was built with the 40,000 most frequent tokens in the corpus (a cut-off point that included all the extracted A-N pairs). The original dimensions were the 3,000 most frequent con-

[1] Mitchell & Lapata (2008) make very similar assumptions to the ones adopted here.

tent words in the BNC. The vector space was reduced to the first 500 "latent" dimensions by SVD as implemented by the *Infomap* software. Thus, the resulting space consists in a matrix with $40,000 \times 500$ dimensions.

We then extracted the vector representation for each A-N candidate as well as for each independent constituent, e.g. vectors for *nice_house* (v3), as well as for *nice* (v1) and *house* (v2) were saved. The resulting vector subspace was imported into the R statistical computing environment for the subsequent model building and evaluation. In particular, we produced our regression analysis with the `pls` package (Mevik & Wehrens, 2007), which implements PLSR and a number of very useful functions for cross-validation, prediction, error analysis, etc.

By simply combining the vector representations of the independent Adjectives and Nouns in our data-set (*v1* and *v2*) we built an additive prediction model ($v1 + v2$) and a simplified pointwise multiplicative prediction model ($v1 \times v2$) for each candidate pair.

We also fitted a PLSR model using *v1* and *v2* as predictors and the corresponding observed pair *v3* as dependent variable. The data were divided into a training set (1,000 A-N pairs) and a testing set (the remaining 380 A-N pairs). The model's parameters were estimated by performing 10-fold cross-validation during the training phase.

In what follows we briefly evaluate the three resulting models of compositionality.

5 Evaluation

In order to evaluate the three models of compositionality that were built, we devised two different procedures based on the Euclidean measure of geometric distance.

The first method draws a direct comparison of the different predicted vectors for each candidate A-N pair by computing the Euclidean distance between the observed vector and the modelled predictions. We also inspect a general distance matrix for the whole compositionality subspace, i.e. all the observed vectors and all the predicted vectors. We extract the 10 nearest neighbours for the 380 Adjective-Noun pairs in the test set and look for the intended predicted vectors in each case. The idea here is that the best models should produce predictions that are as close as possible to the originally observed A-N vector.

Our second evaluation method uses the 10 nearest neighbours of each of the observed A-N pairs in the test set as gold-standard (excluding any modelled predictions), and compares them with the 10 nearest neighbours of each of the corresponding predictions as generated by the models. The aim is to assess if the predictions made by each model share any top-10 neighbours with their corresponding gold-standard. We award 1 point for every shared neighbour.

5.1 The distance of predictions

We calculated the Euclidean distance between each observed A-N pair and the corresponding prediction made by each model. On general inspection, it is clear that the approximation of A-N compositional vectors made by PLSR is considerably closer than those produced by the additive and multiplicative models, cf. Table 1.

	Min.	1st Q.	Median	Mean	3rd Q.	Max.
ADD	0.877	1.402	1.483	1.485	1.570	1.814
MUL	0.973	0.998	1.002	1.002	1.005	1.019
PLSR	0.624	0.805	0.856	0.866	0.919	1.135

Table 1: Summary of distance values between the 380 observed A-N pairs and the predictions from each model (ADD=additive, MUL=multiplicative, PLSR=Partial Least Squares Regression).

We also computed in detail which of the three predicted composed vectors was closest to the corresponding observation. To this effect we extracted the 10 nearest neighbours for each A-N pair in the test set using the whole compositionality subspace (all the predicted and the original vectors). In 94 cases out of 380, the PLSR intended prediction was the nearest neighbour. Cumulatively, PLSR's predictions were in the top-10 nearest neighbour list in 219 out of 380 cases (57.6%). The other models' performance in this test was negligible, cf. Table 2. Overall, 223 items in the test set had at least one predicted vector in the top-10 list; of these, 219 (98%) were generated by PLSR and the remaining 4 (1%) by the multiplicative model.

	1	2	3	4	5	6	7	8	9	10	Tot.
ADD	0	0	0	0	0	0	0	0	0	0	0
MUL	0	1	0	2	1	0	0	0	0	0	4
PLSR	94	51	24	18	10	7	7	5	2	1	219

Table 2: Nearest predicted neighbours and their positions in the top-10 list.

5.2 Comparing prediction neighbours to the gold standard

Since the main use of DSMs is to extract similar vectors from a multidimensional space (representing related documents, distributional synonyms, etc.), we would like to test if the modelling of semantic compositionality is able to produce predictions that are as similar as possible to the originally observed data. A very desirable result would be if any predicted compositional A-N vector could be reliably used instead of the extracted bigram. This could only be achieved if a model's predictions show a similar distributional behaviour with respect to the observed vector.

To test this idea using our data, we took the 10 nearest neighbours of each of the observed A-N pairs in the test set as gold standard. These gold neighbours were extracted from the observation testing subspace, thus excluding any modelled predictions. This is a very restrictive setting: it means that the gold standard for each of the 380 test items is composed of the 10 nearest neighbours from the same 380 items (which may turn out to be not very close at all). We then extracted the 10 nearest neighbours for each of the three modelled predictions, but this time the subspace included all predictions, as well as all the original observations ($380 \times 4 = 1520$ items). Finally, we tested if the predictions made by each model shared any top-10 neighbours with their corresponding gold-standard. We awarded 1 point for every shared neighbour.

The results obtained with these evaluation settings were very poor. Only the additive model scored points (48), although the performance was rather disappointing (maximum potential score for the test was 3,800 points). Both the pointwise multiplicative model and the PLSR model failed to retrieve any of the gold standard neighbours. This poor results can be attributed to the very restrictive nature of our gold standard and, also, to the asymmetrical composition of the compared data (gold standard: 3,800 neighbours from a pool of just 380 different items; prediction space: 11,400 neighbours from a pool of 1,520 items).

However, given the that DSMs are known for their ability to extract similar items from the same space, we decided to relax our test settings by awarding points not only to shared neighbours, but also to the same model's predictions of those neighbours. Thus, given a target neighbour such as *good_deal*, in our second setting we awarded points not only to the gold standard *good_deal*, but also to the predictions *good_deal_ADD*, *good_deal_MUL* and *good_deal_PLSR* when evaluating each corresponding model. With these settings the compared spaces become less asymmetrical (gold standard: 7,600 neighbours from a pool of just 380 different items plus predictions; prediction space: 11,400 neighbours from a pool of 1,520 items). The obtained results show a great improvement (max. potential score 7,600 points):

	Shared Neigh.	Predicted Neigh.	Total
ADD	48	577	625
MUL	0	37	37
PLSR	0	263	263
Not shared:			6,675

Table 3: Shared neighbours with respect to the gold standard and shared predicted neighbours.

Once again, the additive model showed the best performance, followed by PLSR. The multiplicative model's performance was negligible.

While carrying out these experiments, an unexpected fact became evident. Each of the models in turn produces predictions that are relatively close to each other, regardless of the independent words that were used to calculate the compositional vectors. This has the consequence that the nearest neighbour lists for each model's predictions are, by and large, populated by items generated in the same model, as shown in Table 4.

	ADD	MUL	PLSR	OBS
ADD	2,144 (56%)	–	–	–
MUL	59 (1%)	3,800 (100%)	998 (26%)	1,555 (40%)
PLSR	1,472 (38%)	–	2,802 (73%)	2,190 (57%)
OBS	125 (3%)	–	–	55 (1%)

Table 4: Origins of neighbours in each models' top-10 list of neighbours extracted from the full space composed of observations and predictions ($380 \times 4 = 1,440$ items) (ADD=additive, MUL=multiplicative, PLSR=Partial Least Squares Regression, OBS=observed vectors) .

Neighbours of predictions from the multiplicative model are all multiplicative. The additive model has the most varied set of neighbours, but the majority of them are additive-neighbours. PLSR shows a mixed behaviour. However, PLSR produced neighbours that find their way into the neighbour sets of both the additive model and the observations.

These remarks point in the same direction: every model is a simplified and specialised version of the original space, somewhat more orderly than the observed data, and may give different results depending on the task at stake. PLSR (and to a lesser extent also the multiplicative model) is particularly efficient as generator of neighbours for real vectors, a characteristic that could be applied to guess distributional synonyms of unseen A-N pairs. On the other hand, the additive model (and to a lesser extent PLSR) is especially successful in attracting gold standard neighbours. Overall, even at this experimental stage, PLSR is clearly the model that produces the most consistent results.

6 Concluding remarks

This paper proposed a novel method to model the compositionality of meaning in distributional models of semantics. The method, Partial Least Squares Regression, is well known in other data-intensive fields of research, but to our knowledge had never been put to work in computational distributional semantics. Its main advantage is the fact that it is designed to approximate functions in problems of multivariate multiple regression where the number of observations is relatively small if compared to the number of variables (dimensions).

We built a DSM targeting a type of semantic composition that has not been treated extensively in the literature before, adjacent A-N pairs.

The model built by PLSR performed better than both a simple additive model and a multiplicative model in the first proposed evaluation method.

Our second evaluation test (using comparison to a gold standard) gave mixed results: the best performance was obtained by the simple additive model, with PLSR coming in second place.

This is work in progress, but the results look very promising. Future developments will certainly focus on the creation of better evaluation methods, as well as on extending the experiments to other techniques (e.g. convolution product as discussed by Widdows, 2008 and Giesbrecht, 2009). Another important issue that we still have not touched is the role played by lexical association (collocations) in the prediction models. We would like to make sure that we are not modelling the compositionality of non-compositional examples.

A last word on the view of semantic compositionality suggested by our approach. Modelling compositionality as a machine learning task implies that a great number of different "types" of composition (functions combining vectors) may be learned from natural language samples. In principle, any semantic relation instantiated by any syntactic structure could be learned if sufficient data is provided. This approach must be confronted with other linguistic phenomena, also of greater complexity than just a set of bigrams. Finally, we might wonder if there is an upper limit to the number of compositionality functions that we need to learn in natural language, or if there are types of functions that are more difficult, or even impossible, to learn.

Acknowledgements

Thanks are due to Marco Baroni, Stefan Evert, Roberto Zamparelli and the three anonymous reviewers for their assistance and helpful comments.

References

Marco Baroni and Alessandro Lenci. 2009. One semantic memory, many semantic tasks. In *Proceedings GEMS 2009*, 3–11. Athens: Association for Computational Linguistics.

Eugenie Giesbrecht. 2009. In Search of Semantic Compositionality in Vector Spaces. In Proceedings of the 17th International Conference on Conceptual Structures, ICCS 2009, Moscow, Russia, pp. 173–184. Berlin: Springer.

Zellig Harris. 1970 [1954]. Distributional structure. In *Papers in structural and transformational linguistics*, 775–794. Dordrecht: Reidel.

Bjørn-Helge Mevik and Ron Wehrens. 2007. The `pls` package: principal component and partial least squares regression in R. *Journal of Statistical Software*, 18(2): 1–24.

Jeff Mitchell and Mirella Lapata. 2008. Vector-based Models of Semantic Composition. In *Proceedings of ACL-08: HLT*, 236–244. Columbus, OH.

Dominic Widdows. 2008. Semantic Vector Products: Some Initial Investigations. Second AAAI Symposium on Quantum Interaction, Oxford, 26th–28th March 2008. URL: `http://www.puttypeg.com/papers/`

Magnus Sahlgren. 2006. *The Word Space Model*. Ph.D. dissertation, Stockholm University.

Semantic Composition with Quotient Algebras

Daoud Clarke
University of Hertfordshire
Hatfield, UK
daoud@metrica.net

Rudi Lutz
University of Sussex
Brighton, UK
rudil@sussex.ac.uk

David Weir
University of Sussex
Brighton, UK
davidw@sussex.ac.uk

Abstract

We describe an algebraic approach for computing with vector based semantics. The tensor product has been proposed as a method of composition, but has the undesirable property that strings of different length are incomparable. We consider how a quotient algebra of the tensor algebra can allow such comparisons to be made, offering the possibility of data-driven models of semantic composition.

1 Introduction

Vector based techniques have been exploited in a wide array of natural language processing applications (Schütze, 1998; McCarthy et al., 2004; Grefenstette, 1994; Lin, 1998; Bellegarda, 2000; Choi et al., 2001). Techniques such as latent semantic analysis and distributional similarity analyse contexts in which terms occur, building up a vector of features which incorporate aspects of the meaning of the term. This idea has its origins in the distributional hypothesis of Harris (1968), that words with similar meanings will occur in similar contexts, and vice-versa.

However, there has been limited attention paid to extending this idea beyond individual words, so that the distributional meaning of phrases and whole sentences can be represented as vectors. While these techniques work well at the word level, for longer strings, data becomes extremely sparse. This has led to various proposals exploring methods for *composing* vectors, rather than deriving them directly from the data (Landauer and Dumais, 1997; Foltz et al., 1998; Kintsch, 2001; Widdows, 2008; Clark et al., 2008; Mitchell and Lapata, 2008; Erk and Pado, 2009; Preller and Sadrzadeh, 2009). Many of these approaches use a pre-defined composition operation such as addition (Landauer and Dumais, 1997; Foltz et al., 1998) or the tensor product (Smolensky, 1990; Clark and Pulman, 2007; Widdows, 2008) which contrasts with the *data-driven* definition of composition developed here.

2 Tensor Algebras

Following the context-theoretic semantics of Clarke (2007), we take the meaning of strings as being described by a multiplication on a vector space that is bilinear with respect to the addition of the vector space, i.e.

$$x(y+z) = xy + xz \quad (x+y)z = xz + yz$$

It is assumed that the multiplication is associative, but *not* commutative. The resulting structure is an **associative algebra over a field** — or simply an **algebra** when there is no ambiguity.

One commonly used bilinear multiplication operator on vector spaces is the **tensor product** (denoted $\otimes$), whose use as a method of combining meaning was first proposed by Smolensky (1990), and has been considered more recently by Clark and Pulman (2007) and Widdows (2008), who also looked at the **direct sum** (which Widdows calls the direct product, denoted $\oplus$).

We give a very brief account of the tensor product and direct sum in the finite-dimensional case; see (Halmos, 1974) for formal and complete definitions. Roughly speaking, if $u_1, u_2, \ldots u_n$ form an orthonormal basis for a vector space U and $v_1, v_2, \ldots v_m$ form an orthonormal basis for vector space V, then the space $U \otimes V$ has dimensionality nm with an orthonormal basis formed by the set of all ordered pairs (u_i, v_j), denoted by $u_i \otimes v_j$, of the individual basis elements. For arbitrary elements $u = \sum_{i=1}^{n} \alpha_i u_i$ and $v = \sum_{j=1}^{m} \beta_j v_j$ the tensor product of u and v is then given by

$$u \otimes v = \sum_{i}^{n} \sum_{j}^{m} \alpha_i \beta_j \, u_i \otimes v_j$$

Proceedings of the 2010 Workshop on GEometrical Models of Natural Language Semantics, ACL 2010, pages 38–44,
Uppsala, Sweden, 16 July 2010.

For two finite dimensional vector spaces U and V (over a field F) of dimensionality n and m respectively, the direct sum $U \oplus V$ is defined as the cartesian product $U \times V$ together with the operations $(u_1, v_1) + (u_2, v_2) = (u_1 + u_2, v_1 + v_2)$, and $a(u_1, v_1) = (au_1, av_1)$, for $u_1, u_2 \in U$, $v_1, v_2 \in V$ and $a \in F$. In this case the vectors $u_1, u_2, \ldots u_n, v_1, v_2, \ldots v_m$ form an orthonormal set of basis vectors in $U \oplus V$, which is thus of dimensionality $n + m$. In this case one normally identifies U with the set of vectors in $U \oplus V$ of the form $(u, 0)$, and V with the set of vectors of the form $(0, v)$. This construction makes $U \oplus V$ isomorphic to $V \oplus U$, and thus the direct sum is often treated as commutative, as we do in this paper.

The motivation behind using the tensor product to combine meanings is that it is very fine-grained. So, if, for example, *red* is represented by a vector u consisting of a feature for each noun that is modified by *red*, and *apple* is represented by a vector v consisting of a feature for each verb that occurs with *apple* as a direct object, then *red apple* will be represented by $u \otimes v$ with a non-zero component for every pair of non-zero features (one from u and one from v). So, there is a non-zero element for each composite feature, *something that has been described as red*, and *something that has been done with an apple*, for example, *sky* and *eat*.

Both $\oplus$ and $\otimes$ are intuitively appealing as semantic composition operators, since u and v are reconstructible from each of $u \otimes v$ and $u \oplus v$, and thus no information is lost in composing u and v. Conversely, this is not possible with ordinary vector addition, which also suffers from the fact that it is strictly commutative (not simply up to isomorphism like $\oplus$), whereas natural language composition is in general manifestly non-commutative.

We make use of a construction called the **tensor algebra** on a vector space V (where V is a space of context features), defined as:

$$T(V) = \mathbb{R} \oplus V \oplus (V \otimes V) \oplus (V \otimes V \otimes V) \oplus \cdots$$

Any element of $T(V)$ can be described as a sum of components with each in a different tensor power of V. Multiplication is defined as the tensor product on these components, and extended linearly to the whole of $T(V)$. We define the **degree** of a vector u in $T(V)$ to be the tensor power of its highest dimensional non-zero component, and denote it $\deg(u)$; so for example, both $v \otimes v$ and $u \oplus (v \otimes v)$ have degree two, for $0 \neq u, v \in V$. We restrict $T(V)$ to only contain vectors of finite degree.

A standard way to compare elements of a vector space is to make use of an **inner product**, which provides a measure of semantic distance on that space. Assuming we have an inner product $\langle \cdot, \cdot \rangle$ on V, $T(V)$ can be given an inner product by defining $\langle \alpha, \beta \rangle = \alpha\beta$ for $\alpha, \beta \in \mathbb{R}$, and

$$\langle x_1 \otimes y_1, x_2 \otimes y_2 \rangle = \langle x_1, x_2 \rangle \langle y_1, y_2 \rangle$$

for $x_1, y_1, x_2, y_2 \in V$, and then extending this inductively (and by linearity) to the whole of $T(V)$.

We assume that words are associated with vectors in V, and that the higher tensor powers represent strings of words. The problem with the tensor product as a method of composition, given the inner product as we have defined it, is that strings of different lengths will have orthogonal vectors, clearly a serious problem, since strings of different lengths can have similar meanings. In our previous example, the vector corresponding to the concept *red apple* lives in the vector space $U \otimes V$, and so we have no way to compare it to the space V of nouns, even though *red apple* should clearly be related to *apple*.

Previous work has not made full use of the tensor product space; only tensor products are used, not sums of tensor products, giving us the equivalent of the **product states** of quantum mechanics. Our approach imposes relations on the vectors of the tensor product space that causes some product states to become equivalent to **entangled states**, containing sums of tensor products of different degrees. This allows strings of different lengths to share components. We achieve this by constructing a **quotient algebra**.

3 Quotient Algebras

An **ideal** I of an algebra A is a sub-vector space of A such that $xa \in I$ and $ax \in I$ for all $a \in A$ and all $x \in I$. An ideal introduces a congruence $\equiv$ on A defined by $x \equiv y$ if and only if $x - y \in I$. For any set of elements $\Lambda \subseteq A$ there is a unique minimal ideal I_Λ containing all elements of Λ; this is called the ideal **generated** by Λ. The quotient algebra A/I is the set of all equivalence classes defined by this congruence. Multiplication is defined on A/I by the multiplication on A, since $\equiv$ is a congruence.

By adding an element $x - y$ to the generating set Λ of an ideal, we are saying that we want to set $x - y$ to zero in the quotient algebra, which has the effect of setting x equal to y. Thus, if we have a set of pairs of vectors that we wish to make equal in the quotient algebra, we put their differences in the generating set of the ideal. Note that putting a single vector v in the generating set can have knock-on effects, since all products of v with elements of A will also end up in the ideal.

Although we have an inner product defined on $T(V)$, we are not aware of any satisfactory method for defining an inner product on $T(V)/I$, a consequence of the fact that both $T(V)$ and I are not complete. Instead, we define an inner product on a space which contains the quotient algebra, $T(V)/I$. Rather than considering all elements of the ideal when computing the quotient, we consider a sub-vector space of the ideal, limiting ourselves to the space G_k generated from Λ by only allowing multiplication by elements up to a certain degree, k.

Let us denote the vector subspace generated by linearity alone (no multiplications) from a subset Λ of $T(V)$ by $G(\Lambda)$. Also suppose $B = \{e_1, \ldots, e_N\}$ is a basis for V. We then define the spaces G_k as follows. Define sets Λ_k ($k = 0, 1, 2, \ldots$) inductively as follows:

$$\Lambda_0 = \Lambda$$

$$\Lambda_k = \Lambda_{k-1} \cup \{(e_i \otimes \Lambda_{k-1}) | e_i \in B\} \cup \{(\Lambda_{k-1} \otimes e_i) | e_i \in B\}$$

Define

$$G_k = G(\Lambda_k)$$

We note that

$$G_0 \subseteq G_1 \subseteq \ldots G_k \subseteq \ldots \subseteq I \subseteq T(V)$$

form an increasing sequence of linear vector subspaces of $T(V)$, and that

$$I = \bigcup_{k=0}^{\infty} G_k$$

This means that for any $x \in I$ there exists a smallest k such that for all $k' \geq k$ we have that $x \in G_{k'}$.

Lemma. *Let $x \in I, x \neq 0$ and let $\deg(x) = d$. Then for all $k \geq d - mindeg(\Lambda)$ we have that $x \in G_k$, where $mindeg(\Lambda)$ is defined to be the minimum degree of the non-zero components occurring in the elements of Λ.*

Proof. We first note that for $x \in I$ it must be the case that $\deg(x) \geq mindeg(\Lambda)$ since I is generated from Λ. Therefore we know $d - mindeg(\Lambda) \geq 0$. We only need to show that $x \in G_{d-mindeg(\Lambda)}$. Let k' be the smallest integer such that $x \in G_{k'}$. Since $x \notin G_{k'-1}$ it must be the case that the highest degree term of x comes from $V \otimes G_{k'-1} \cup G_{k'-1} \otimes V$. Therefore $k' + mindeg(\Lambda) \leq d \leq k' + maxdeg(\Lambda)$. From this it follows that the smallest k' for which $x \in G_{k'}$ satisfies $k' \leq d - mindeg(\Lambda)$, and we know $x \in G_k$ for all $k \geq k'$. In particular $x \in G_k$ for $k \geq d - mindeg(\Lambda)$. □

We show that $T(V)/G_k$ (for an appropriate choice of k) captures the essential features of $T(V)/I$ in terms of equivalence:

Proposition. *Let $\deg(a - b) = d$ and let $k \geq d - mindeg(\Lambda)$. Then $a \equiv b$ in $T(V)/G_k$ if and only if $a \equiv b$ in $T(V)/I$.*

Proof. Since $G_k \subseteq I$, the equivalence class of an element a in $T(V)/I$ is a superset of the equivalence class of a in $T(V)/G_k$, which gives the forward implication. The reverse follows from the lemma above. □

In order to define an inner product on $T(V)/G_k$, we make use of the result of Berberian (1961) that if M is a finite-dimensional linear subspace of a pre-Hilbert space P, then $P = M \oplus M^{\perp}$, where $M^{\perp}$ is the orthogonal complement of M in P. In our case this implies $T(V) = G_k \oplus G_k^{\perp}$ and that every element $x \in T(V)$ has a unique decomposition as $x = y + x'_k$ where $y \in G_k$ and $x'_k \in G_k^{\perp}$. This implies that $T(V)/G_k$ is isomorphic to $G_k^{\perp}$, and that for each equivalence class $[x]_k$ in $T(V)/G_k$ there is a unique corresponding element $x'_k \in G_k^{\perp}$ such that $x'_k \in [x]_k$. This element x'_k can be thought of as the **canonical representation** of all elements of $[x]_k$ in $T(V)/G_k$, and can be found by projecting any element in an equivalence class onto $G_k^{\perp}$. This enables us to define an inner product on $T(V)/G_k$ by $\langle [x]_k, [y]_k \rangle_k = \langle x'_k, y'_k \rangle$.

The idea behind working in the quotient algebra $T(V)/I$ rather than in $T(V)$ is that the elements of the ideal capture differences that we wish to ignore, or alternatively, equivalences that we wish to impose. The equivalence classes in $T(V)/I$ represent this imposition, and the canonical representatives in $I^{\perp}$ are elements which ignore the distinctions between elements of the equivalence classes.

However, by using G_k, for some k, instead of the full ideal I, we do not capture some of the equivalences implied by I. We would, therefore, like to choose k so that no equivalences of importance *to the sentences we are considering* are ignored. While we have not precisely established a minimal value for k that achieves this, in the discussion that follows, we set k heuristically as

$$k = l - mindeg(\Lambda)$$

where l is the maximum length of the sentences currently under consideration, and Λ is the generating set for the ideal I. The intuition behind this is that we wish all vectors occurring in Λ to have some component in common with the vector representation of our sentences. Since components in the ideal are generated by multiplication (and linearity), in order to allow the elements of Λ containing the lowest degree components to potentially interact with our sentences, we will have to allow multiplication of those elements (and all others) by components of degree up to $l - mindeg(\Lambda)$.

Given a finite set $\Lambda \subseteq T(V)$ of elements generating the ideal I, to compute canonical representations, we first compute a generating set Λ_k for G_k following the inductive definition given earlier, and removing any elements that are not linearly independent using a standard algorithm. Using the Gram-Schmidt process (Trefethen and Bau, 1997), we then calculate an orthonormal basis Λ' for G_k, and, by a simple extension of Gram-Schmidt, compute the projection of a vector u onto $G_k^\perp$ using the basis Λ'.

We now show how Λ, the set of vectors generating the ideal, can be constructed on the basis of a tree-bank, ensuring that the vectors for any two strings of the same grammatical type are comparable.

4 Data-driven Composition

Suppose we have a tree-bank, its associated tree-bank grammar G, and a way of associating a context vector with every occurrence of a subtree in the tree-bank (where the vectors indicate the presence of features occurring in that particular context). The context vector associated with a specific occurrence of a subtree in the tree-bank is an **individual** context vector.

We assume that for every rule, there is a distinguished non-terminal on the right hand side which we call the head. We also assume that for every production π there is a linear function ϕ_π from the space generated by the individual context vectors of the head to the space generated by the individual context vectors of the left hand side. When there is no ambiguity, we simply denote this function ϕ.

Let $\widehat{X}$ be the sum over all individual vectors of subtrees rooted with X in the tree-bank. Similarly, for each X_j in the right-hand-side of the rule $\pi_i : X \rightarrow X_1 \ldots X_{r(\pi_i)}$, where $r(\pi)$ is the rank of π, let $\widehat{\pi_{i,j}}$ be the sum over the individual vectors of those subtrees rooted with X_j where the subtree occurs as the jth daughter of a local tree involving the production π_i in the tree-bank.

For each rule $\pi : X \rightarrow X_1 \ldots X_r$ with head X_h we add vectors

$$\lambda_{\pi,i} = \phi(e_i) - \widehat{X}_1 \otimes \ldots \otimes \widehat{X}_{h-1} \otimes e_i \otimes \widehat{X}_{h+1} \otimes \ldots \otimes \widehat{X}_r$$

for each basis element e_i of V_{X_h} to the generating set. The reasoning behind this is to ensure that the meaning corresponding to a vector associated with the head of a rule is maintained as it is mapped to the vector space associated with the left hand side of the rule.

It is often natural to assume that the individual context vector of a non-terminal is the same as the individual context vector of its head. In this case, we can take ϕ to be the identity map. In particular, for a rule of the form $\pi : X \rightarrow X_1$, then $\lambda_{\pi,i}$ is zero.

It is important to note at this point that we have presented only one of many ways in which a grammar could be used to generate an ideal. In particular, it is possible to add more vectors to the ideal, allowing more fine-grained distinctions, for example through the use of a lexicalised grammar.

For each sentence w, we compute the tensor product $\hat{w} = \hat{a}_1 \otimes \hat{a}_2 \otimes \cdots \otimes \hat{a}_n$ where the string of words $a_1 \ldots a_n$ form w, and each $\hat{a}_i$ is a vector in V. For a sentence w we find an element $\hat{w}_O$ of the orthogonal complement of G_k in $T(V)$ such that $\hat{w}_O \in [\hat{w}]$, where $[\hat{w}]$ denotes the equivalence class of $\hat{w}$ given the subspace G_k.

5 Example

We show how our formalism applies in a simple example. Assume we have a corpus which consists of the following sentences:

	apple	*big apple*	*red apple*	*city*	*big city*	*red city*	*book*	*big book*	*red book*
apple	1.0	0.26	0.24	0.52	0.13	0.12	0.33	0.086	0.080
big apple		1.0	0.33	0.13	0.52	0.17	0.086	0.33	0.11
red apple			1.0	0.12	0.17	0.52	0.080	0.11	0.33
city				1.0	0.26	0.24	0.0	0.0	0.0
big city					1.0	0.33	0.0	0.0	0.0
red city						1.0	0.0	0.0	0.0
book							1.0	0.26	0.24
big book								1.0	0.33
red book									1.0

Figure 1: Similarities between phrases

see red apple
buy apple
read big book
throw old small red book
buy large new book
see big city
visit big apple
modernise city
see modern city

together with the following productions.

1. $N' \to \text{Adj } N'$
2. $N' \to N$

where N and Adj are terminals representing nouns and adjectives, along with rules for the terminals. We consider the space of adjective/noun phrases, generated by N', and define the individual context of a noun to be the verb it occurs with, and the individual context of an adjective to be the noun it modifies. For each rule, we take ϕ to be the identity map, so the vector spaces associated with N and N', and the vector space generated by individual contexts of the nouns are all the same. In this case, the only non-zero vectors which we add to the ideal are those for the second rule (ignoring the first rule, since we do not consider verbs in this example except as contexts), which has the set of vectors

$$\lambda_i = e_i - \widehat{\text{Adj}} \otimes e_i$$

where i ranges over the basis vectors for contexts of nouns: see, buy, $visit$, $read$, $modernise$, and

$$\widehat{\text{Adj}} = 2e_{apple} + 2e_{book} + e_{city}$$

In order to compute canonical representations of vectors, we take $k = 1$.

5.1 Discussion

Figure 1 shows the similarity between the noun phrases in our sample corpus. Note that the vectors we have put in the generating set describe only compositionality of meaning — thus for example the similarity of the non-compositional phrase *big apple* to *city* is purely due to the distributional similarity between *apple* and *city* and composition with the adjective *big*.

Our preliminary investigations indicate that the cosine similarity values are very sensitive to the particular corpus and features chosen; we are currently investigating other ways of measuring and computing similarity.

One interesting feature in the results is how adjectives alter the similarity between nouns. For example, *red apple* and *red city* have the same similarity as *apple* and *city*, which is what we would expect from a pure tensor product. This also explains why all phrases containing *book* are disjoint to those containing *city*, since the original vector for *book* is disjoint to *city*.

The contribution that the quotient algebra gives is in comparing the vectors for nouns with those for noun-adjective phrases. For example, *red apple* has components in common with *apple*, as we would expect, which would not be the case with just the tensor product.

6 Conclusion and Further Work

We have presented the outline of a novel approach to semantic composition that uses quotient algebras to compare vector representations of strings of different lengths.

The dimensionality of the construction we use increases exponentially in the length of the sentence; this is a result of our use of the tensor product. This causes a problem for computation using longer phrases; we hope to address this in future work by looking at the representations we use. For example, product states can be represented in much lower dimensions by representing them as products of lower dimensional vectors.

The example we have given would seem to indicate that we intend putting abstract (syntactic) information about meaning into the set of generating elements of the ideal. However, there is no reason that more fine-grained aspects of meaning cannot be incorporated, even to the extent of putting in vectors for every pair of words. This would automatically incorporate information about non-compositionality of meaning. For example, by including the vector $\widehat{big\ apple} - \widehat{big} \otimes \widehat{apple}$, we would expect to capture the fact that the term *big apple* is non-compositional, and more similar to *city* than we would otherwise expect.

Future work will also include establishing the implications of varying the constant k and exploring different methods for choosing the set Λ that generates the ideal. We are currently preparing an experimental evaluation of our approach, using vectors obtained from large corpora.

7 Acknowledgments

We are grateful to Peter Hines, Stephen Clark, Peter Lane and Paul Hender for useful discussions. The first author also wishes to thank Metrica for supporting this research.

References

Jerome R. Bellegarda. 2000. Exploiting latent semantic information in statistical language modeling. *Proceedings of the IEEE*, 88(8):1279–1296.

Sterling K. Berberian. 1961. *Introduction to Hilbert Space*. Oxford University Press.

Freddy Choi, Peter Wiemer-Hastings, and Johanna Moore. 2001. Latent Semantic Analysis for text segmentation. In *Proceedings of the 2001 Conference on Empirical Methods in Natural Language Processing*, pages 109–117.

Stephen Clark and Stephen Pulman. 2007. Combining symbolic and distributional models of meaning. In *Proceedings of the AAAI Spring Symposium on Quantum Interaction*, pages 52–55, Stanford, CA.

Stephen Clark, Bob Coecke, and Mehrnoosh Sadrzadeh. 2008. A compositional distributional model of meaning. In *Proceedings of the Second Quantum Interaction Symposium (QI-2008)*, pages 133–140, Oxford, UK.

Daoud Clarke. 2007. *Context-theoretic Semantics for Natural Language: an Algebraic Framework*. Ph.D. thesis, Department of Informatics, University of Sussex.

Katrin Erk and Sebastian Pado. 2009. Paraphrase assessment in structured vector space: Exploring parameters and datasets. In *Proceedings of the EACL Workshop on Geometrical Methods for Natural Language Semantics (GEMS)*.

P. W. Foltz, W. Kintsch, and T. K. Landauer. 1998. The measurement of textual coherence with latent semantic analysis. *Discourse Process*, 15:285–307.

Gregory Grefenstette. 1994. *Explorations in automatic thesaurus discovery*. Kluwer Academic Publishers, Dordrecht, NL.

Paul Halmos. 1974. *Finite dimensional vector spaces*. Springer.

Zellig Harris. 1968. *Mathematical Structures of Language*. Wiley, New York.

W. Kintsch. 2001. Predication. *Cognitive Science*, 25:173–202.

T. K. Landauer and S. T. Dumais. 1997. A solution to Plato's problem: the latent semantic analysis theory of acquisition, induction and representation of knowledge. *Psychological Review*, 104(2):211–240.

Dekang Lin. 1998. Automatic retrieval and clustering of similar words. In *Proceedings of the 36th Annual Meeting of the Association for Computational Linguistics and the 17th International Conference on Computational Linguistics (COLING-ACL '98)*, pages 768–774, Montreal.

Diana McCarthy, Rob Koeling, Julie Weeds, and John Carroll. 2004. Finding predominant word senses in untagged text. In *ACL '04: Proceedings of the 42nd Annual Meeting on Association for Computational Linguistics*, page 279, Morristown, NJ, USA. Association for Computational Linguistics.

Jeff Mitchell and Mirella Lapata. 2008. Vector-based models of semantic composition. In *Proceedings of ACL-08: HLT*, pages 236–244, Columbus, Ohio, June. Association for Computational Linguistics.

Anne Preller and Mehrnoosh Sadrzadeh. 2009. Bell states and negation in natural languages. In *Proceedings of Quantum Physics and Logic*.

Heinrich Schütze. 1998. Automatic word sense discrimination. *Computational Linguistics*, 24(1):97–123.

Paul Smolensky. 1990. Tensor product variable binding and the representation of symbolic structures in connectionist systems. *Artificial Intelligence*, 46(1-2):159–216, November.

Lloyd N. Trefethen and David Bau. 1997. *Numerical Linear Algebra*. SIAM.

Dominic Widdows. 2008. Semantic vector products: Some initial investigations. In *Proceedings of the Second Symposium on Quantum Interaction, Oxford, UK*.

Expectation Vectors: A Semiotics Inspired Approach to Geometric Lexical-Semantic Representation

Justin Washtell
University of Leeds
Leeds, UK
washtell@comp.leeds.ac.uk

Abstract

We introduce a new family of geometric models of meaning, inspired by principles from semiotics and information theory, based on what we call Expectation Vectors. We present theoretical arguments in support of these representations over traditional context-feature vectors: primarily that they provide a more intuitive representation of meaning, and detach vector representation from the specific context features thereby allowing arbitrarily sophisticated language models to be leveraged. We present a preliminary evaluation of an expectation vector based word sense disambiguation system using the SemEval-2007 task 2 dataset, with very encouraging results, particularly with respect to ambiguous verbs.

1 Introduction

It is a cornerstone assumption of distributional lexical semantics that the distribution of words in a corpus reflects their meaning. Common interpretations of this include the Distributional Hypothesis (Harris, 1954) and the Contextual Hypotheses (Miller & Charles, 1991), which state that there is a relationship between a word's meaning, and the context(s) in which it appears. In recent years this insight has been borne out by correlations between human judgements and distributional models of word similarity (Rapp, 2002), and steady advances in tasks such as word sense disambiguation (Schütze, 1998) and information retrieval. The workhorse of these approaches are wordspace models: vectors built from context features which serve as geometric analogues of meaning. Despite many advances, substantial problems exist with this approach to modelling meaning. Amongst these are the problems of data sparseness and of how to model compositional meaning.

In this short paper, we introduce a new family of wordspace models, based on insights gleaned from semiotics and information theory, called Expectation Vectors. These retain the convenient vector-based paradigm whilst encouraging the exploitation of advances in language modelling from other areas of NLP. We finish by outlining some present efforts to evaluate expectation vectors in the area of word sense disambiguation.

2 Modelling meaning from context

Perhaps one of the most prominent application areas to exploit context-based wordspace models is that of word sense induction and disambiguation (WSI/WSD). The prevailing approach to this problem is based on a fairly literal interpretation of the Distributional Hypothesis: that is to cluster or classify instances of ambiguous words according to certain features of the context in which they appear – invariably other words. It is not difficult to see why this approach is limiting: as Pedersen (2008) observes, *"the unifying thread that binds together many short context applications and methods is the fact that similarity decisions must be made between contexts that share few (if any) words in common."* This is a manifestation of what is commonly referred to at the data sparseness problem, and it pervades all of corpus-based NLP. This problem is exacerbated as available examples of a word sense decrease, or finer sense granularities are sought. For supervised tasks this implies that a large training set is required, which is often expensive. For unsupervised tasks, such as WSI, it has negative implications for cluster quality and rule learning. Consequently, Leacock *et al* (1996) observe that WSD systems which operate directly upon context are: *"plagued with the same problem, excellent precision but low recall"*.

"Backing off" to more general feature classes through say lemmatization or part-of-speech tagging affords one way of alleviating sparseness (Joshi & Penstein-Rosé, 2009), assuming these features are pertinent to the task. Similar strategies include the use of dual-context models where immediate lexical features are backed up by more general topical ones garnered from the wider context of the ambiguous word (Leacock *et al*, 1996; Yarowsky, 1993).

Others have tackled the problem of sparseness without recourse to generalized feature classes,

Proceedings of the 2010 Workshop on GEometrical Models of Natural Language Semantics, ACL 2010, pages 45–50, Uppsala, Sweden, 16 July 2010. ©2010 Association for Computational Linguistics

through the exploitation of higher-order distributional information. Schütze (1998) popularised this approach within the WSD/WSI task. Rather than comparing contexts directly, it is the distributional similarity of those features (in the corpus) which are compared. Specifically, Schütze composed context vectors by summing the vectors for every word in a context, where those vectors were themselves formed from the total of word co-occurrence counts pertaining to every instance of that word in the corpus. The resultant context vectors are therefore comparatively dense, and carry second-order information which makes otherwise unlike contexts more amenable to comparison. One contention of this model is that it conflates co-occurrence information from all occurrences of a word in the corpus, regardless of their sense. The defence is that because the actual senses of the term instances which appear in the context of the ambiguous word will tend to be pertinent to that word's own specific sense, it is that common aspect of their respective conflated-sense vectors - when summed - which will dominant the resultant context vector. Purandare & Pedersen (2001) performed a comparative study of disambiguation approaches based on first-order context, and on second order context as per Schütze (1998). They found that while Schütze's approach provided gains when data was limited, when the training corpus was large enough that sufficient examples existed, clustering on first order context was actually a better approach. This suggests that while alleviating the data-sparseness problem, the practice of expanding context vectors in this way introduces a certain amount of noise, presumably by inappropriately over-smoothing the data.

Another approach to the sparse data problem which was also part of Schütze's framework is dimensionality reduction by Singular Value Decomposition (SVD). In SVD the set of context features are analytically combined and reduced in a manner that exploits their latent similarities, whereafter traditional vector measures can be used. Very similar techniques to both of those used by Schütze have been used for query expansion and document representation in information retrieval (Qiu & Frei, 1993; Xu *et al*, 2007).

Several variations upon Schütze's approach to WSD have been explored. Dagan *et al* (1995) and Karov & Edelman (1996) both apply what they call "similarity-based" methods which, while markedly different on the surface to that of Schütze, are similar in spirit and intent. Karov & Edelman, for example, use machine-readable dictionary glosses as opposed to corpus-derived co-occurrences, and apply an iterative bootstrapping approach to augment the available data, rather than strict second-order information.

Typically, context vectors comprise a component (dimension) for each designated feature in a word's context. In a simple bag-of-words model this might equate to one vector component for each potential word that can appear in the context. For more sophisticated n-gram or dependency-based models, which attempt to better capture the structure inherent in the language, this number of vector components must be increased. The more sophisticated the language model becomes therefore, the more acute the sparse data problem. Techniques like SVD can reduce this sparseness, but other issues remain. How does one weight heterogeneous features when forming a vector? How does one interpret vectors reduced by SVD? Looking at the variety of approaches to tackling the problem, we might be forgiven for questioning whether representing meaning as a vector of context features is in fact an ideal starting point for semantic tasks such as WSD.

In the following section we describe a means of entirely detaching context feature selection from vector representation, such that an arbitrarily sophisticated language model can be used to generate dense, comparable vectors. Necessarily, we also present a prototype distributional language model that will serve as the basis of our investigations into this approach.

3 System & approach

3.1 Lexical Expectation Vectors

Theoretical motivation. The motivation behind the method presented herein comes both from the fields of semiotics and information theory. It is the notion that the "meaning" of an utterance is not in the utterance itself, nor in its individual or typical context; it is in the *disparity* between our expectations based on that context, and the utterance (Noth, 1990; Chandler, 2002). Meaning in this sense can be seen as related to information (Attneave, 1959; Shannon, 1948): an utterance which is entirely expected under a regime where speaker and interpreter have identical frames of reference communicates nothing; conversely an extremely creative utterance is laden with information, and may have multiple non-obvious interpretations (poetry being a case in point - Riffaterre, 1978). This idea is also lent some weight by psycholinguistic experiments which have revealed correlations between a word's disparity from its preceding context, and processing times in human subjects. Similar insights have been employed in some very recent attempts to model compositional word meaning Erk & Padó (2008) and Thater *et al* (2009). These models augment word and context representations with additional vectors encoding the selectional preferences (expectations) pertaining to the specific syntactic/semantic roles of the participating words. So far these systems rely upon parsed corpora and have been tested only with very limited contexts (e.g. pairs of words having specific dependency relations).

Lexical expectation vectors are based on a similar and very simple premise: rather than building a vector for a context by conflating the features which comprise the various context words (as per Schutze, 1998), we instead conflate all the words which might be expected to appear *within the context* (i.e. in the headword position). Consider the following short context taken from the SemEval-2007 task 2 dataset:

```
Mr. Meador takes responsibility
for <?> and property management .
```

The strongest twenty elements of its expectation vector (as generated by the system described below) are shown in table 1. The figures represent some measure of confidence that a given word will be found in the headword position <?>.

0.42	education	0.31	chancellor
0.38	forms	0.31	routine
0.36	housing	0.31	health
0.35	counselling	0.31	research
0.35	these	0.31	assessment
0.35	herself	0.3	detailed
0.34	database	0.3	management
0.33	injuries	0.3	many
0.32	advice	0.3	training
0.31	this	0.3	what

Table 1: An example of an expectation vector.

We make the supposition that when the vectors implied by the respective likelihoods of *all words* implied by two contexts are identical, the contexts can be considered semantically equivalent.[1] Note that the actual headword appearing in the context is not taken into consideration for the purposes of calculating expectation. In this example it occur at rank 62 out of ~650,000, implying that its use in this context is not atypical.

Formal approach. For the purpose of our present research, we adopt the following formal framework for generating an expectation vector. Given a context c, each component of the expectation vector $\mathbf{e}$ arising from that context is estimated thusly:

$$\mathbf{e}_j = P(j|c) \sim \max_{o_j^k \in O_j} \operatorname{sim}(o_j^k, c)$$

Where j is a given word type in the lexicon, O_j is the set of all observed contexts of that word type in some corpus, o_j^k is the kth observed context of that word type, and $\operatorname{sim}(o,c)$ is some similarity measure between two contexts.

The process of generating an expectation vector can be thought of as a kind of transform from *syntagmatic* space, into *paradigmatic* space. This mapping need not be trivial: items which are close in the syntagmatic space need not be close in the paradigmatic space and vice-versa (although in practice we expect some considerable correlation by virtue of the distributional hypothesis). Note that although our work herein assumes a popular vector representation of context, the nature of the contexts and the similarity measure which operates upon them are not constrained in any way by the framework given above. For example they may equally well be dependency trees.

In the following section we outline a distance-based language model comprising a context model and a similarity metric which operates upon it. This choice of model allows us to maintain a purely distributional approach without suffering the data-sparseness associated with n-gram models.

3.2 Language model

Theoretical motivation. The precise relationship between syntagmatic and paradigmatic spaces implied by the expectation transform depends upon the language model employed. In a naive language model which assumes independence between features, this mapping can be fully represented by a square matrix over word types. Although such models are the mainstay of many systems in NLP, adopting the toolset of an expection transform in such a case gains us little. Therefore the relevance of the approach to the present task depends wholly upon having a suitably sophisticated language model.

Building on the work of Washtell (2009) and Terra & Clarke (2004), a distance-based language model is used in the present work. This is in contrast to the bag-of-words, n-gram, or syntactic dependency models more commonly described in the NLP literature. There are two hypothesised advantages to this approach. Firstly, this avoids the issue of immediate context versus wider topical

[1] Equivalent with respect to the head of the context. This is not the same as saying the passages have the same meaning, which requires recourse to compositionality.

context. While immediate context is generally accepted to play a dominant role in WSD, both near and far context have been shown to be useful - the specific balance being somewhat dependent on the ambiguous word in question (Yarowsky, 1993; Gale et al, 1992; Leacock *et al*, 1996). As Ide & Veronis (1998) astutely observe, "*although a distinction is made between micro-context and topical context in current WSD work, it is not clear that this distinction is meaningful. It may be more useful to regard the two as lying along a continuum, and to consider the role and importance of contextual information as a function of distance from the target.*" This is precisely the assumption adopted herein. Secondly, the use of distance-based information alleviates data sparseness. This is simply by virtue of the fact that all words types in a document form part of a token's context (barring document boundaries, no cut-off distance is imposed). Moreover, as it is specific distance information which is being recorded, rather than (usually low) frequency counts, context vector components and the similarity measurements which arise from them exhibit good precision. Washtell (2009) showed that these properties of distance-based metrics lead to measurable gains in information extracted from a corpus. In the context of modelling human notions of association this also led to improved predictive power (Washtell & Markert, 2009).

Formal approach. We do not pre-compute any statistical representation of the data upon which our language model draws. With available approaches this would either require throwing away a large number of potentially relevant higher-order dependencies, or would otherwise be intractable. Our intuition is that the truest representation of the language encoded in the corpus is the corpus itself. We therefore use an indexed corpus directly for all queries.

We use the following as a prototype measure of structural similarity (see section 3.1), although note that others are by all means possible.

$$\mathrm{sim}(\mathbf{o},\mathbf{c}) = \frac{\sum_{\{p,q\}\subseteq O\cap C} f(\mathbf{o}_p, \mathbf{o}_q, \mathbf{c}_p, \mathbf{c}_q)}{\min(|O|, |C|)^2}$$

Where **o** and **c** are context vectors whose j components each specify the position in the text of the nearest occurrence (to the head of the context) of a given word type. O and C are the set of indices of all non-zero (i.e. observed) components in **o** and **c** respectively. The head of the context is represented by an additional component in vectors **o** and **c**, and is always treated as observed. f is a further function of the positions of words p and q in both contexts. It returns a similarity score in the unit range designating how similar the distance $\mathbf{o}_p\leftrightarrow\mathbf{o}_q$ is to that of $\mathbf{c}_p\leftrightarrow\mathbf{c}_q$.

The more consistent the relative positions of the various symbols comprising two contexts, the stronger their similarity. Note that the measure is additive: symbols which occur at all in both contexts result in positive score contributions. We assume that a context is usually incomplete (i.e. that that which lies outside it is unknown, rather than non-existent). The minimum operator in the denominator (the normalization factor) therefore ensures that words present only in the larger of two contexts do not constitute negative evidence.

This formulation allows for considerable leeway in how word distances are represented and compared. In this work we choose to treat distances proportionately, so small variations in word position between distant (presumably topically related words) are tolerated better than similar distance variations between neighbouring (more syntactico-semantically related) words.

4 Word Sense Disambiguation

A WSD system based on expectation vectors was ineligible in the SemEval-2010 WSI/WSD task by virtue of restrictions disallowing the use of a corpus-based language model. Instead, this task implicitly encouraged participants to focus on context feature selection and clustering approaches. It seems unlikely to us that these stages are where the major bottlenecks for WSD (or WSI) lie; performing WSD on short contexts without any extra-contextual information (i.e. general linguistic or domain experience) is arguably not a task which even humans could be expected to perform well. For this reason we have chosen to focus initially on the well explored SemEval-2007 task 2 dataset.

4.1 Preliminary Evaluation

An expectation vector was produced for each training and test instance in the SemEval dataset by matching the headword's context against that of each word position in the British National Corpus using an implementation of the distance based similarity measure outlined in section 3.2. For matters of convenience, independent forwards and backwards expectation vectors were produced from the context preceding the headword and that following it, and their elements were multiplied together to produce the final vector. No lemmatization or part-of-speech tagging was employed. Neither was any dimensionality reduction, each vector therefore having ~650,000 elements: one for each word type in the corpus.

Each test sample's vector was compared against all corresponding training sample vectors using both cosine similarity and Euclidean distance[2]. In the MAX setups (see Table 2), each test case was assigned the sense of the single nearest training example according to the metric being used. In the CosOR setup, sense scores were generated by applying a probabilistic OR operation over the squared Cosine similarities of *all* relevant training examples[3]. The BaseMFS setup is a popular baseline in which the most frequent sense in the training set for a given ambiguous word is attributed to every test case.

	Nouns	Verbs	All
CosMAX	**83.6** ▲6.1 ▼22.8	**70.5** ▲7.6 ▼14.4	**79.5** ▲6.7 ▼19.5
EucMAX	78.9	67.0	75.1
CosOR	83.5	66.1	78.0
BaseMFS	78.8	65.5	74.5

Table 2: Recall on SemEval WSD task, including relative performance gain (▲) and error reduction (▼) over baseline for best setup (preliminary based on first 25% of test cases).

	Nouns	Verbs	All
BEST	**86.8** ▲7.3 ▼30.9	**76.2** ▲0.0 ▼0.0	**81.6** ▲3.7 ▼13.6
BaseMFS	80.9	76.2	78.7

Table 3: Recall of best official SemEval WSD systems (Agirre & Soroa, 2007), showing relative performance gain and error reduction over baseline.

Table 2 shows the results for each test case in terms of recall, for all words and for nouns and verbs separately. Also shown in table 3 are the best and baseline figures for the official entries from the Semeval workshop. Note that figures are not directly comparable between tables because our preliminary results represent only the first 25% of the SemEval dataset (hence the different baselines). To aid some comparison, figures are included in both tables indicating the relative increases in recall over the baseline, and relative reduction in error. Note that the system employed here is not a word sense induction system as were most of those participating in the official SemEval task. The setup of the tasks however allows for systems which perform poorly under the induction evaluation to perform competitively as disambiguation systems, so we are not precluded from making meaningful comparisons here.

5 Discussion and Future Direction

We have presented a new type of wordspace model based on vectors derived from the predictions of a language model applied to a context, rather than directly from the features of a context itself. We have conducted a preliminary investigation of the semantic modelling power of such vectors in the setting of a popular WSD task. The results are very encouraging. Although it is too early to draw hard conclusions, preliminary results suggest a performance at least comparable the present state of the art on this task. What is particularly noteworthy is that the approach taken here seems to perform equally well at discriminating verbs and nouns. Verbs have traditionally proven very problematic: *none* of the six SemEval systems were able to improve upon the verb baseline. More recent studies have focused on discriminating nouns (Brody & Lapata, 2009; Klapaftis & Manandhar, 2007).

Further gains might be expected by employing a corpus which is more closely matched to the material being disambiguated, such as the Wall Street Journal in the present case.

It is also worth noting that the system presented here was aided only by an untagged un-lemmatised corpus, without the use of any structured knowledge sources. While we expect that judicious use of lemmatization could improve these results, we believe the key to the quality of expectation vectors is in the specific predictive language model employed. We have scarcely experimented with this, opting for a relatively untested distance-based model throughout, and choosing instead to experiment with the application of different vector similarity measures. While the nature of the language model used enables it to capture complex interdependencies, and long-range dependencies, it is based on direct querying of a corpus and therefore does not scale at all well. This makes its use in the context of most applications or with larger corpora untenable. Exploring alternative language models (drawing upon the copious research in this field) is therefore a focus for future research; the ability to do this highlights one of the major advantages of this approach to modelling meaning.

[2] Cosine Similarity captures the similarity between the relative proportions of features present in each of two vectors. By contrast, Euclidean Distance compares the actual values of corresponding features.

[3] Although encountered rarely in the literature, squared Cosine Similarity is a pertinent quantity for tasks that go beyond simple ranking. As with Pearson's R^2, it represents the degree or proportion of similarity (consider that the square of an angle's cosine and that of its sine total 1).

References

Eneko Agirre, Airotr Soroa, 2007, *SemEval-2007 Task 02: Evaluating Word Sense Induction and Discrimination Systems*

Fred Attneave, *Applications of Information Theory to Psychology: A Summary of Basic Concepts, Methods, and Results,* Holt, New York

Samuel Brody, Mirella Lapata, 2009, *Bayesian Word Sense Induction,* Proceedings of EACL 2009, pages 103-111

Daniel Chandler, 2002, *Semiotics: The Basics*, p88, Routleadge

Ido Dagan, Shaul Marcus, Shaul Markovitch, 1995, *Contextual Word Similarity and Estimation from Sparse Data,* Proceedings of 31st ACL, pages 164-171

Katrin Erk, Sebastian Padó, 2008, *A Structured Vector Space Model for Word Meaning in Context*, Proceedings on EMNLP 2008

William Gale, Kenneth Church, , David Yarowsky, *1992, A Method for Disambiguating Word Senses in a Large Corpus, Computers and the Humanities,* 26, 415-429

Zellig Harris, 1954, *Distributional structure.* Word, 10(23), pages 146-162

Nancy Ide, Jean Veronis, 1998, *Word Sense Disambiguation: The State of The Art,*

Mahesh Joshi, Carolyn Penstein-Rosé, 2009, *Generalizing Dependency Features for Opinion Mining*, Proceeding of the ACL-IJCNLP 2009 Conference Short Papers, pages 313-316

Yael Karov, Shimon Edelman, 1996, *Learning Similarity-Based Word Sense Disambiguation from Sparse Data*

Ioannis Klapaftis, Suresh Manandhar, 2008, *Word Sense Induction using Graphs of Collocations,* Proceedings of ECAI 2008, pages 298-302

Claudia Leacock, Geoffrey Towell, Ellen M. Voorhees, 1996, *Towards Building Contextual Representations of Word Senses Using Statistical Models.* In B. Boguraev and H.Pustejovsky (eds) Corpus Processing for Lexical Acquisition. MIT Press, pages 97-113

G. A. Miller, W. G Charles, 1991. *Contextual correlates of semantic similarity.* Language and Cognitive Processes, *6*, 1-28.

Winfried Noth, 1990, *Handbook of Semiotics*, Indiana University Press, p 142

Reinhard Rapp. 2002. *The computation of word associations: comparing syntagmatic and paradigmatic approaches.* In Proceedings of the 19th international Conference on Computational Linguistics.

Hinrich Schütze, 1998, *Automatic Word Sense Discrimination*, Computational Linguistics, 24(1), pages 97-123

Ted Pedersen, 2008, *Computational Approaches to Measuring the Similarity of Short Contexts: A Review of Applications and Methods,* to appear

Amruta Purandare, Ted Pederson, 2004, *Word sense discrimination by clustering contexts in vector and similarity spaces.* Proceeding of the Conference on Computational Natural Language Learning, pages 41-48

Yonggang Qiu, Hans-Peter Frei, 1993, Proceedings of the 16th annual international ACM SIGIR conference on Research and development in information retrieval table of contents, 160-169

Miachael Riffaterre, 1978, *Semiotics Of Poetry*, Methuen

Hae Jong Seo, Peyman Milanfar, 2009, *Training-free, Generic Object Detection using Locally Adaptive Regression Kernels*, IEEE Transactions on Pattern Analysis and Machine Intelligence, 99

Claude E Shannon, 1948, *A Mathematical Theory of Communication*, Bell System Technical Journal, vol. 27, pages 379-423, 623-656,

Egidio Terra, Charles L. A. Clarke, 2004, *Fast computation of lexical affinity models* , Proceedings of the 20th international conference on Computational Linguistics

Stefan Thater, Georgiana Dinu, Manfred Pinkal, 2009, *Ranking Paraphrases in Context,* Proceedings of the 2009 Workshop on Applied Textual Inference, pages 44-47

Justin Washtell. 2009. *Co-dispersion: A windowless approach to lexical association.* In Proceedings of EACL-2009.

Justin Washtell, Katja Markert. 2009. *Comparing windowless and window-based computational association measures as predictors of syntagmatic human associations.* In Proceedings of EMNLP-2009, pages 628-637.

Xuheng Xu, Xiaodan Zhang, Xiaohua Hu, 2007, *Using Two-Stage Concept-Based Singular Value Decomposition Technique as a Query Expansion Strategy,* AINAW'07

David Yarowsky, 1993, *One Sense Per Collocation,* Proceedings on the Workshop on Human Language Technology, pages 266-271

Sketch Techniques for Scaling Distributional Similarity to the Web

Amit Goyal, Jagadeesh Jagarlamudi, Hal Daumé III, and Suresh Venkatasubramanian
School of Computing
University of Utah
Salt Lake City, UT 84112
{amitg, jags, hal, suresh}@cs.utah.edu

Abstract

In this paper, we propose a memory, space, and time efficient framework to scale distributional similarity to the web. We exploit sketch techniques, especially the Count-Min sketch, which approximates the frequency of an item in the corpus without explicitly storing the item itself. These methods use hashing to deal with massive amounts of the streaming text. We store all item counts computed from 90 GB of web data in just 2 billion counters (8 GB main memory) of CM sketch. Our method returns semantic similarity between word pairs in $O(K)$ time and can compute similarity between any word pairs that are stored in the sketch. In our experiments, we show that our framework is as effective as using the exact counts.

1 Introduction

In many NLP problems, researchers (Brants et al., 2007; Turney, 2008) have shown that having large amounts of data is beneficial. It has also been shown that (Agirre et al., 2009; Pantel et al., 2009; Ravichandran et al., 2005) having large amounts of data helps capturing the semantic similarity between pairs of words. However, computing distributional similarity (Sec. 2.1) between word pairs from large text collections is a computationally expensive task. In this work, we consider scaling distributional similarity methods for computing semantic similarity between words to Web-scale.

The major difficulty in computing pairwise similarities stems from the rapid increase in the number of unique word-context pairs with the size of text corpus (number of tokens). Fig. 1 shows that

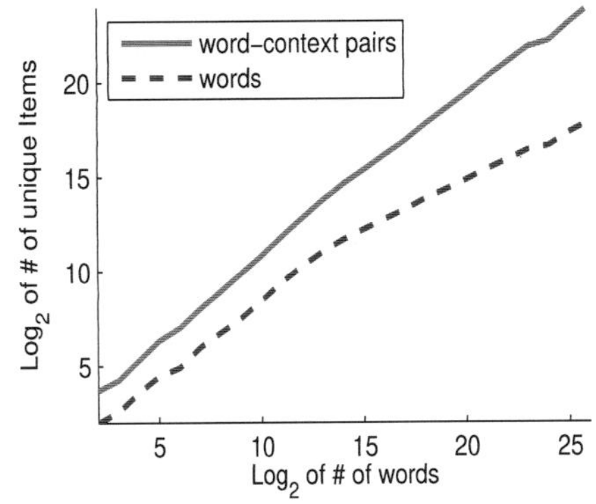

Figure 1: Token Type Curve

the number of unique word-context pairs increase rapidly compared to the number words when plotted against the number of tokens[1]. For example, a 57 million word corpus[2] generates 224 thousand unique words and 15 million unique word-context pairs. As a result, it is computationally hard to compute counts of all word-context pairs with a giant corpora using conventional machines (say with main memory of 8 GB). To overcome this, Agirre et al. (2009) used MapReduce infrastructure (with 2,000 cores) to compute pairwise similarities of words on a corpus of roughly 1.6 Terawords.

In a different direction, our earlier work (Goyal et al., 2010) developed techniques to make the computations feasible on a conventional machines by willing to accept some error in the counts. Similar to that work, this work exploits the idea of Count-Min (CM) sketch (Cormode and Muthukrishnan, 2004) to approximate the frequency of word pairs in the corpus without explicitly storing the word pairs themselves. In their, we stored

[1] Note that the plot is in log-log scale.

[2] 'Subset' column of Table 1 in Section 5.1

Proceedings of the 2010 Workshop on GEometrical Models of Natural Language Semantics, ACL 2010, pages 51–56,
Uppsala, Sweden, 16 July 2010.

counts of all words/word pairs in fixed amount of main memory. We used conservative update with CM sketch (referred as CU sketch) and showed that it reduces the average relative error of its approximate counts by a factor of two. The approximate counts returned by CU Sketch were used to compute approximate PMI between word pairs. We found their that the approximate PMI values are as useful as the exact PMI values for computing semantic orientation (Turney and Littman, 2002) of words. In addition, our intrinsic evaluations in their showed that the quality of approximate counts and approximate PMI is good.

In this work, we use CU-sketch to store counts of items (words, contexts, and word-context pairs) using fixed amount of memory of 8 GB by using only $2B$ *counters*. These approximate counts returned by CU Sketch are converted into approximate PMI between word-context pairs. The top K contexts (based on PMI score) for each word are used to construct distributional profile (DP) for each word. The similarity between a pair of words is computed based on the cosine similarity of their respective DPs.

The above framework of using CU sketch to compute semantic similarity between words has five good properties. First, this framework can return semantic similarity between any word pairs that are stored in the CU sketch. Second, it can return the similarity between word pairs in time O(K). Third, because we do not store items explicitly, the overall space required is significantly smaller. Fourth, the additive property of CU sketch (Sec. 3.2) enables us to parallelize most of the steps in the algorithm. Thus it can be easily extended to very large amounts of text data. Fifth, this easily generalizes to any kind of association measure and semantic similarity measure.

2 Background

2.1 Distributional Similarity

Distributional Similarity is based on the distributional hypothesis (Firth, 1968; Harris, 1985) that words occur in similar contexts tend to be similar. The context of a word is represented by the distributional profile (DP), which contains the strength of association between the word and each of the lexical, syntactic, semantic, and/or dependency units that co-occur with it[3]. The association is commonly measured using conditional probability, pointwise mutual information (PMI) or log likelihood ratios. Then the semantic similarity between two words, given their DPs, is calculated using similarity measures such as Cosine, α-skew divergence, and Jensen-Shannon divergence. In our work, we use PMI as association measure and cosine similarity to compute pairwise similarities.

2.2 Large Scale NLP problems

Pantel et al. (2009) computed similarity between 500 million word pairs using the MapReduce framework from a 200 billion word corpus using 200 quad-core nodes. The inaccessibility of clusters for every one has attracted NLP community to use streaming, and randomized algorithms to handle large amounts of data.

Ravichandran et al. (2005) used locality sensitive hash functions for computing word-pair similarities from large text collections. Their approach stores a enormous matrix of all unique words and their contexts in main memory which makes it hard for larger data sets. In our work, we store all unique word-context pairs in CU sketch with a pre-defined size[4].

Recently, the streaming algorithm paradigm has been used to provide memory and time-efficient platform to deal with terabytes of data. For example, we (Goyal et al., 2009); Levenberg and Osborne (2009) build approximate language models and show their effectiveness in SMT. In (Van Durme and Lall, 2009b), a TOMB Counter (Van Durme and Lall, 2009a) was used to find the top-K verbs "y" with the highest PMI for a given verb "x". The idea of TOMB is similar to CU Sketch. However, we use CU Sketch because of its simplicity and attractive properties (see Sec. 3). In this work, we go one step further, and compute semantic similarity between word-pairs using approximate PMI scores from CU sketch.

2.3 Sketch Techniques

Sketch techniques use a sketch vector as a data structure to store the streaming data compactly in a small-memory footprint. These techniques use hashing to map items in the streaming data onto a small sketch vector that can be easily updated and queried. These techniques generally process the input stream in one direction, say from left to right,

[3]In this work, we only consider lexical units as context.

[4]We use only 2 billion counters which takes up to 8 GB of main memory.

without re-processing previous input. The main advantage of using these techniques is that they require a storage which is significantly smaller than the input stream length. A survey by (Rusu and Dobra, 2007; Cormode and Hadjieleftheriou, 2008) comprehensively reviews the literature.

3 Count-Min Sketch

The Count-Min Sketch (Cormode and Muthukrishnan, 2004) is a compact summary data structure used to store the frequencies of all items in the input stream.

Given an input stream of items of length N and user chosen parameters δ and ϵ, the algorithm stores the frequencies of all the items with the following guarantees:

- All reported frequencies are within ϵN of true frequencies with probability of atleast δ.
- Space used by the algorithm is $O(\frac{1}{\epsilon}\log\frac{1}{\delta})$.
- Constant time of O(log($\frac{1}{\delta}$)) per each update and query operation.

3.1 CM Data Structure

A Count-Min Sketch with parameters (ϵ,δ) is represented by a two-dimensional array with width w and depth d :

$$\begin{bmatrix} \text{sketch}[1,1] & \cdots & \text{sketch}[1,w] \\ \vdots & \ddots & \vdots \\ \text{sketch}[d,1] & \cdots & \text{sketch}[d,w] \end{bmatrix}$$

Among the user chosen parameters, ϵ controls the amount of tolerable error in the returned count and δ controls the probability with which the returned count is not within this acceptable error. These values of ϵ and δ determine the width and depth of the two-dimensional array respectively. To achieve the guarantees mentioned in the previous section, we set w=$\frac{2}{\epsilon}$ and d=log($\frac{1}{\delta}$). The depth d denotes the number of pairwise-independent hash functions employed by the algorithm and there exists an one-to-one correspondence between the rows and the set of hash functions. Each of these hash functions h_k:$\{x_1 \ldots x_N\} \rightarrow \{1 \ldots w\}$, $1 \leq k \leq d$ takes an item from the input stream and maps it into a counter indexed by the corresponding hash function. For example, $h_2(x) = 10$ indicates that the item "x" is mapped to the 10th position in the second row of the sketch array. These d hash functions are chosen uniformly at random from a pairwise-independent family.

Initialize the entire sketch array with zeros.

Update Procedure: When a new item "x" with count c arrives[5], one counter in each row, as decided by its corresponding hash function, is updated by c. Formally, $\forall 1 \leq k \leq d$

$$\text{sketch[k,}h_k(x)] \leftarrow \text{sketch[k,}h_k(x)] + c$$

Query Procedure: Since multiple items can be hashed to the same counter, the frequency stored by each counter is an overestimate of the true count. Thus, to answer the point query, we consider all the positions indexed by the hash functions for the given item and return the minimum of all these values. The answer to Query(x) is: $\hat{c} = \min_k$ sketch$[k, h_k(x)]$.

Both update and query procedures involve evaluating d hash functions. Hence, both these procedures are linear in the number of hash functions. In our experiments (see Section5), we use d=3 similar to our earlier work (Goyal et al., 2010). Hence, the update and query operations take only constant time.

3.2 Properties

Apart from the advantages of being space efficient and having constant update and querying time, the CM sketch has other advantages that makes it attractive for scaling distributional similarity to the web:

1. Linearity: given two sketches s_1 and s_2 computed (using the same parameters w and d) over different input streams, the sketch of the combined data stream can be easily obtained by adding the individual sketches.
2. The linearity allows the individual sketches to be computed independent of each other. This means that it is easy to implement it in distributed setting, where each machine computes the sketch over a subset of the corpus.

3.3 Conservative Update

Estan and Varghese introduce the idea of conservative update (Estan and Varghese, 2002) in the context of networking. This can easily be used with CM Sketch (CU Sketch) to further improve the estimate of a point query. To update an item, w with frequency c, we first compute the frequency $\hat{c}$ of

[5] In our setting, c is always 1.

this item from the existing data structure and the counts are updated according to: $\forall 1 \leq k \leq d$

$$\text{sketch[k,}h_k(x)] \leftarrow \max\{\text{sketch[k,}h_k(x)], \hat{c} + \text{c}\}$$

The intuition is that, since the point query returns the minimum of all the d values, we will update a counter only if it is necessary as indicated by the above equation. This heuristic avoids the unnecessary updating of counter values and thus reduces the error.

4 Efficient Distributional Similarity

To compute distributional similarity efficiently, we store counts in CU sketch. Our algorithm has three main steps:

1. Store approximate counts of all words, contexts, and word-context pairs in CU-sketch using fixed amount of counters.
2. Convert these counts into approximate PMI scores between word-context pairs. Use these PMI scores to store top K contexts for a word on the disk. Store these top K context vectors for every word stored in the sketch.
3. Use cosine similarity to compute the similarity between word pairs using these approximate top K context vectors constructed using CU sketch.

5 Word pair Ranking Evaluations

As discussed earlier, the DPs of words are used to compute similarity between a pair of words. We used the following four test sets and their corresponding human judgements to evaluate the word pair rankings.

1. **WS-353**: WordSimilarity-353[6] (Finkelstein et al., 2002) is a set of 353 word pairs.
2. **WS-203**: A subset of WS-353 containing 203 word pairs marked according to similarity[7] (Agirre et al., 2009).
3. **RG-65**: (Rubenstein and Goodenough, 1965) is set of 65 word pairs.
4. **MC-30**: A smaller subset of the RG-65 dataset containing 30 word pairs (Miller and Charles, 1991).

[6]http://www.cs.technion.ac.il/ gabr/resources/data/wordsim353/wordsim353.html

[7]http://alfonseca.org/pubs/ws353simrel.tar.gz

Each of these data sets come with human ranking of the word pairs. We rank the word pairs based on the similarity computed using DPs and evaluate this ranking against the human ranking. We report the spearman's rank correlation coefficient (ρ) between these two rankings.

5.1 Corpus Statistics

The Gigaword corpus (Graff, 2003) and a copy of the web crawled by (Ravichandran et al., 2005) are used to compute counts of all items (Table. 1). For both the corpora, we split the text into sentences, tokenize, convert into lower-case, remove punctuations, and collapse each digit to a symbol "0" (e.g. "1996" gets collapsed to "0000"). We store the counts of all words (excluding numbers, and stop words), their contexts, and counts of word-context pairs in the CU sketch. We define the context for a given word "x" as the surrounding words appearing in a window of 2 words to the left and 2 words to the right. The context words are concatenated along with their positions -2, -1, +1, and +2. We evaluate ranking of word pairs on three different sized corpora: Gigaword (GW), GigaWord + 50% of web data (GW-WB1), and GigaWord + 100% of web data (GW-WB2).

Corpus	**Sub set**	**GW**	**GW-WB1**	**GW-WB2**
Size (GB)	.32	9.8	49	90
# of sentences (Million)	2.00	56.78	462.60	866.02
Stream Size (Billion)	.25	7.65	37.93	69.41

Table 1: Corpus Description

5.2 Results

We compare our system with two baselines: Exact and Exact1000 which use exact counts. Since computing the exact counts of all word-context pairs on these corpora is not possible using main memory of only 8 GB , we generate context vectors for only those words which appear in the test set. The former baseline uses all possible contexts which appear with a test word, while the latter baseline uses only the top 1000 contexts (based on PMI value) for each word. In each case, we use a cutoff (of 10, 60 and 120) on the frequency of word-context pairs. These cut-offs were selected based on the intuition that, with more data, you get more noise, and not considering word-context pairs with frequency less than 120 might be a bet-

Data	GW			GW-WB1			GW-WB2		
Model	Frequency cutoff			Frequency cutoff			Frequency cutoff		
	10	60	120	10	60	120	10	60	120
		ρ			ρ			ρ	
				WS-353					
Exact	.25	.25	**.22**	.29	.28	.28	.30	.28	.28
Exact1000	.36	**.28**	**.22**	**.46**	.43	.37	**.47**	**.44**	.41
Our Model	**.39**	**.28**	**.22**	-0.09	**.48**	**.40**	-0.03	.04	**.47**
				WS-203					
Exact	.35	.36	.33	.38	.38	.37	.40	.38	.38
Exact1000	**.49**	**.40**	**.35**	**.57**	.55	**.47**	**.56**	**.56**	.52
Our Model	**.49**	**.39**	**.35**	-0.08	**.58**	**.47**	-0.06	.03	**.55**
				RG-65					
Exact	**.21**	**.12**	**.08**	.42	**.28**	.22	.39	**.31**	.23
Exact1000	.14	.09	**.08**	**.45**	.16	.13	**.47**	.26	.12
Our Model	.13	**.10**	**.09**	-0.06	**.32**	.18	-0.05	.08	**.31**
				MC-30					
Exact	.26	**.23**	**.21**	.45	.33	.31	.46	.39	.29
Exact1000	.27	.18	**.21**	**.63**	.42	.32	**.59**	**.47**	.36
Our Model	**.36**	.20	**.21**	-0.08	**.52**	**.39**	-0.27	-0.29	**.52**

Table 2: Evaluating word pairs ranking with Exact and CU counts. Scores are evaluated using ρ metric.

ter choice than a cutoff of 10. The results are shown in Table 2

From the above baseline results, first we learn that using more data helps in better capturing the semantic similarity between words. Second, it shows that using top (K) 1000 contexts for each target word captures better semantic similarity than using all possible contexts for that word. Third, using a cutoff of 10 is optimal for all different sized corpora on all test-sets.

We use approximate counts from CU sketch with *depth*=3 and 2 billion ($2B$) counters ('Our Model')[8]. Based on previous observation, we restrict the number of contexts for a target word to 1000. Table 2 shows that using CU counts makes the algorithm sensitive to frequency cutoff. However, with appropriate frequency cutoff for each corpus, approximate counts are nearly as effective as exact counts. For GW, GW-WB1, and GW-WB2, the frequency cutoffs of 10, 60, and 120 respectively performed the best. The reason for dependence on frequency cutoffs is due to the overestimation of low-frequent items. This is more pronounced with bigger corpus (GW-WB2) as the size of CU sketch is fixed to $2B$ counters and stream size is much bigger (69.41 billion) compared to GW where the stream size is 7.65 billion.

The advantages of using our model is that the sketch contains counts for all words, contexts, and word-context pairs stored in fixed memory of 8 GB by using only $2B$ counters. Note that it is not feasible to keep track of exact counts of all word-context pairs since their number increases rapidly with increase in data (see Fig. 1). We can use our model to create context vectors of size K for all possible words stored in the Sketch and computes semantic similarity between two words in O(K) time. In addition, the linearity of sketch allows us to include new incoming data into the sketch without building the sketch from scratch. Also, it allows for parallelization using the MapReduce framework. We can generalize our framework to any kind of association and similarity measure.

[8]Our goal is not to build the best distributional similarity method. It is to show that our framework scales easily to large corpus and it is as effective as exact method.

6 Conclusion

We proposed a framework which uses CU Sketch to scale distributional similarity to the web. It can compute similarity between any word pairs that are stored in the sketch and returns similarity between them in O(K) time. In our experiments, we show that our framework is as effective as using the exact counts, however it is sensitive to the frequency cutoffs. In future, we will explore ways to make this framework robust to the frequency cutoffs. In addition, we are interested in exploring this framework for entity set expansion problem.

Acknowledgments

We thank the anonymous reviewers for helpful comments. This work is partially funded by NSF grant IIS-0712764 and Google Research Grant Grant for Large-Data NLP.

References

Eneko Agirre, Enrique Alfonseca, Keith Hall, Jana Kravalova, Marius Paşca, and Aitor Soroa. 2009. A study on similarity and relatedness using distributional and wordnet-based approaches. In *NAACL '09: Proceedings of HLT-NAACL.*

Thorsten Brants, Ashok C. Popat, Peng Xu, Franz J. Och, and Jeffrey Dean. 2007. Large language models in machine translation. In *Proceedings of the 2007 Joint Conference on Empirical Methods in Natural Language Processing and Computational Natural Language Learning (EMNLP-CoNLL).*

Graham Cormode and Marios Hadjieleftheriou. 2008. Finding frequent items in data streams. In *VLDB.*

Graham Cormode and S. Muthukrishnan. 2004. An improved data stream summary: The count-min sketch and its applications. *J. Algorithms.*

Cristian Estan and George Varghese. 2002. New directions in traffic measurement and accounting. *SIGCOMM Comput. Commun. Rev.*, 32(4).

L. Finkelstein, E. Gabrilovich, Y. Matias, E. Rivlin, Z. Solan, G. Wolfman, and E. Ruppin. 2002. Placing search in context: The concept revisited. In *ACM Transactions on Information Systems.*

J. Firth. 1968. A synopsis of linguistic theory 1930-1955. In F. Palmer, editor, *Selected Papers of J. R. Firth.* Longman.

Amit Goyal, Hal Daumé III, and Suresh Venkatasubramanian. 2009. Streaming for large scale NLP: Language modeling. In *North American Chapter of the Association for Computational Linguistics (NAACL).*

Amit Goyal, Jagadeesh Jagarlamudi, Hal Daumé III, and Suresh Venkatasubramanian. 2010. Sketching techniques for Large Scale NLP. In *6th Web as Corpus Workshop in conjunction with NAACL-HLT.*

D. Graff. 2003. English Gigaword. Linguistic Data Consortium, Philadelphia, PA, January.

Z. Harris. 1985. Distributional structure. In J. J. Katz, editor, *The Philosophy of Linguistics*, pages 26–47. Oxford University Press, New York.

Abby Levenberg and Miles Osborne. 2009. Stream-based randomised language models for SMT. In *Proceedings of EMNLP*, August.

G.A. Miller and W.G. Charles. 1991. Contextual correlates of semantic similarity. *Language and Cognitive Processes*, 6(1):1–28.

Patrick Pantel, Eric Crestan, Arkady Borkovsky, Ana-Maria Popescu, and Vishnu Vyas. 2009. Web-scale distributional similarity and entity set expansion. In *Proceedings of EMNLP.*

Deepak Ravichandran, Patrick Pantel, and Eduard Hovy. 2005. Randomized algorithms and nlp: using locality sensitive hash function for high speed noun clustering. In *ACL '05: Proceedings of the 43rd Annual Meeting on Association for Computational Linguistics.*

H. Rubenstein and J.B. Goodenough. 1965. Contextual correlates of synonymy. *Computational Linguistics*, 8:627–633.

Florin Rusu and Alin Dobra. 2007. Statistical analysis of sketch estimators. In *SIGMOD '07*. ACM.

P.D. Turney and M.L. Littman. 2002. Unsupervised learning of semantic orientation from a hundred-billion-word corpus.

Peter D. Turney. 2008. A uniform approach to analogies, synonyms, antonyms, and associations. In *Proceedings of COLING 2008.*

Benjamin Van Durme and Ashwin Lall. 2009a. Probabilistic counting with randomized storage. In *IJCAI'09: Proceedings of the 21st international jont conference on Artifical intelligence.*

Benjamin Van Durme and Ashwin Lall. 2009b. Streaming pointwise mutual information. In *Advances in Neural Information Processing Systems 22.*

Active Learning for Constrained Dirichlet Process Mixture Models

Andreas Vlachos
Computer Laboratory
University of Cambridge
av308@cl.cam.ac.uk

Zoubin Ghahramani
Department of Engineering
University of Cambridge
zoubin@eng.cam.ac.uk

Ted Briscoe
Computer Laboratory
University of Cambridge
ejb@cl.cam.ac.uk

Abstract

Recent work applied Dirichlet Process Mixture Models to the task of verb clustering, incorporating supervision in the form of *must-links* and *cannot-links* constraints between instances. In this work, we introduce an active learning approach for constraint selection employing uncertainty-based sampling. We achieve substantial improvements over random selection on two datasets.

1 Introduction

Bayesian non-parametric mixture models have the attractive property that the number of components used to model the data is not fixed in advance but is determined by the model and the data. This property is particularly interesting for NLP where many tasks are aimed at discovering novel information. Recent work has applied such models to various tasks with promising results, e.g. Teh (2006) and Cohn et al. (2009).

Vlachos et al. (2009) applied the basic model of this class, the Dirichlet Process Mixture Model (DPMM), to lexical-semantic verb clustering with encouraging results. The task involves discovering classes of verbs similar in terms of their syntactic-semantic properties (e.g. MOTION class for *travel, walk, run*, etc.). Such classes can provide important support for other tasks, such as word sense disambiguation, parsing and semantic role labeling. (Dang, 2004; Swier and Stevenson, 2004) Although some fixed classifications are available these are not comprehensive and are inadequate for specific domains.

Furthermore, Vlachos et al. (2009) used a constrained version of the DPMM in order to guide clustering towards some prior intuition or considerations relevant to the specific task at hand. This supervision was modelled as pairwise constraints between instances and it informs the model of relations between them that cannot be recovered by the model on the basis of the feature representation used. Like other forms of supervision, these constraints require manual annotation and it is important to maximize the benefits obtained from it. Therefore it is natural to consider active learning (Settles, 2009) in order to focus the supervision on clusterings on which the model is uncertain.

In this work, we propose a simple yet effective active learning method employing uncertainty based sampling. The effectiveness of the AL method is demonstrated on two datasets, one of which has multiple gold standards.

2 Constrained DPMMs for clustering

In DPMMs, the parameters of each component are generated by a Dirichlet Process (DP) which can be seen as a distribution over distributions. Each instance, represented by its features, is generated by the component it is assigned to. The components discovered correspond to the clusters. The prior probability of assigning an instance to a particular component is proportionate to the number of instances already assigned to it, in other words, the DPMM exhibits the "rich get richer" property. A popular metaphor to describe the DPMM which exhibits an equivalent clustering property is the Chinese Restaurant Process (CRP). Customers (instances) arrive at a Chinese restaurant which has an infinite number of tables (components). Each customer sits at one of the tables that is either occupied or vacant with popular tables attracting more customers.

Following Navarro et al. (2006), parameter estimation is performed using Gibbs sampling by sampling the assignment z_i of each instance x_i given all the others z_{-i} and the data X:

$$P(z_i = z|z_{-i}, X) \propto$$
$$p(z_i = z|z_{-i})P(x_i|z_i = z, X_{-i}) \quad (1)$$

Proceedings of the 2010 Workshop on GEometrical Models of Natural Language Semantics, ACL 2010, pages 57–61,
Uppsala, Sweden, 16 July 2010.

In Eq. 1 $p(z_i = z|z_{-i})$ is the CRP prior and $P(x_i|z_i = z, X_{-i})$ is the distribution that generates instance x_i given it has been assigned to component z. This sampling scheme is possible because the assignments in the model are exchangeable, i.e. their order is not relevant.

The constrained version of the DPMM uses pairwise constraints over instances in order to adapt the clustering discovered. Following Wagstaff & Cardie (2000), a pair of instances is either linked together (*must-link*) or not (*cannot-link*). For example, *charge* and *run* should form a *must-link* if the aim is to cluster MOTION verbs together, but they should form a *cannot-link* if we are interested in BILL verbs. All links are assumed to be consistent with each other. In order to incorporate the constraints in the DPMM, the Gibbs sampling scheme is modified so that *must-linked* instances are generated by the same component and *cannot-linked* instances always by different ones. Following Vlachos et al. (2009), for each instance that does not belong to a *linked-group*, the sampler is restricted to choose components that do not contain instances *cannot-linked* with it. For instances in a *linked-group*, their assignment is sampled jointly, again taking into account their *cannot-links*. This is performed by adding each instance of the *linked-group* successively to the same component. In terms of the CRP metaphor, customers connected with *must-links* arrive at the restaurant and choose a table jointly, respecting their *cannot-links* with other customers.

3 Active Constraint Selection

In active learning, the model selects the supervision to be provided by a human expert. In the context of the DPMMs, the model chooses a pair of instances for which a *must-link* or a *cannot-link* must be provided. To select the pair, we employ the simple but effective idea of uncertainty based sampling. We consider the most informative link as that on which the model is most uncertain, more formally the link between instances l^*_{ij} that maximizes the following entropy:

$$l^*_{ij} = \arg\max_{i,j} H(z_i = z_j) \tag{2}$$

If we consider clustering as binary classification of links into *must-links* and *cannot-links*, it is equivalent to selecting the pair with the highest label entropy. During the sampling process used for parameter inference, component assignments vary between samples and the components themselves are not identifiable, i.e. one cannot match the components of one sample with those of another. Furthermore, the conditional assignments estimated during Gibbs sampling (Eq. 1) they do not capture the uncertainty of the assignments z_{-i} on which they condition. Therefore, we resort to generating a set of samples from the (possibly constrained) DPMM and pick the link on which these samples maximally disagree, i.e. we approximate the distribution in Eq. 2 with the probability that instances i, j are in the same cluster or not. Thus, in a given set of samples the most uncertain link would be the one between two instances which are in the same cluster in exactly half of these samples. Using multiple samples allows us to take into account the uncertainty in the assignments of the other instances, as well as the varying number of components.

Compared to standard pool-based AL, when clustering with constraints the possible links between two instances (ignoring transitivity) are $C(N, 2) = N(N-1)/2$ (N is the size of the dataset) and there is an equal number of candidate queries to be considered, as opposed to N queries in a supervised classification task. Another interesting difference is that the the AL process can be initiated without any supervision, since the DPMM is unsupervised. On the other hand, in the standard AL scenario a (usually small) labelled seed set is used. Therefore, we rely exclusively on the model and the features to guide the constraint selection process. If the model combined with the features is not appropriate for the task then the constraints chosen are unlikely to be useful.

4 Datasets and Evaluation

In our experiments we used two verb clustering datasets, one from general English (Sun et al., 2008) and one from the biomedical domain (Korhonen et al., 2006). In both datasets the features for each verb are its subcategorization frames (SCFs) which capture the syntactic context in which it occurs. They were acquired automatically using a domain-independent statistical parsing toolkit, RASP (Briscoe and Carroll, 2002), and a classifier which identifies verbal SCFs. As a consequence, they include some noise due to standard text processing and parsing errors and due to the subtlety of the argument-adjunct distinction. The general English dataset contains 204 verbs belonging to 17 fine-grained classes in Levin's (Levin, 1993) taxonomy so that each class contains 12 verbs. The biomedical dataset consists of 193 medium to high frequency verbs from a corpus of 2230 full-text articles from 3 biomedical journals. A team of linguists and biologists created a three-level gold standard with 16, 34 and 50 classes. Both datasets were pre-processed using non-negative matrix factorization (Lin, 2007) which decomposes a large sparse matrix into two dense matrices (of lower dimensionality) with non-negative values. In all experiments 35 dimensions were kept. Preliminary experiments with different number of dimensions kept did not affect the performance substantially.

We evaluate our results using three information theoretic measures: Variation of Information (Meilă, 2007), V-measure (Rosenberg and Hirschberg, 2007) and V-beta (Vlachos et al., 2009). All three assess the two desirable properties that a clustering should have with respect to a gold standard, homogeneity and completeness. Homogeneity reflects the degree to which each cluster contains instances from a single class and is defined as the conditional entropy of the class distribution of the gold standard given the clustering. Completeness reflects the degree to which each class is contained in a single cluster and is defined as the conditional entropy of clustering given the class distribution in the gold standard. V-beta balances these properties explicitly by taking into account the ratio of the number of cluster discovered over the number of classes in the gold standard. While an ideal clustering should have both properties, naively improving one of them can be harmful for the other. Compared to the more commonly used F-measure (Fung et al., 2003), these measures have the advantage that they do not assume a mapping between clusters and classes.

5 Experiments

We performed experiments in order to assess the effectiveness of the AL algorithm for the constrained DPMM comparing it to random selection. In each AL round, we run the Gibbs sampler for the (constrained) DPMM five times, using 100 iterations for burn-in, draw 20 samples from each run with 5 iterations lag between samples and select the most uncertain link to be labeled. Following Navarro et al. (2006), the concentration parameter is inferred from the data using Gibbs sampling. The performances were averaged across the collected samples. Random selection was repeated three times. The three levels of the biomedical gold standard were used independently and together with the general English dataset result in four experimental setups.

The comparison between AL and random selection for each dataset is shown in graphs 1(a)-1(d) using V-beta, noting that the observations made hold with all evaluation metrics used. Constraints selected via AL improve the performance rapidly. Indicatively, the performance reached using 1000 randomly chosen constraints is obtained using only 110 actively selected ones in the *bio-50* dataset. AL performance levels out in later stages with performance superior to the one achieved using random selection with the same number of constraints. The poor performance of random selection is expected, since the unsupervised DPMM predicts more than 90% of the binary links correctly. Another interesting observation is that, during AL, homogeneity increased faster than completeness (graphs 1(g) and 1(h)). This suggests that the features used lead the model towards finer-grained clusters, which is further confirmed by the fact that the highest scores on the biomedical dataset are achieved when comparing against the finest-grained version of the gold standard. While it is possible to choose constraints to the model that would increase completeness with respect to the gold standard, we argue that this would not allow us to obtain obtain insights on the model and the features used.

We also noticed that the choice of batch size has a significant effect on the learning rate of the model. This phenomenon occurs in varying degrees in many applications of AL. Manual inspection of the links chosen at each round revealed that batches often contained links involving the same instances. This is expected due to transitivity: if the link between instances A and B is uncertain but the link between instances B and C is certain, then the link between A and C will be uncertain too. While reducing the batch size leads to better learning rates, it requires estimating the model more often. In order to ameliorate this issue, after obtaining the label of the most uncertain link, we remove the samples that disagreed with it and re-calculate the uncertainty of the remaining links given the remaining samples. This is repeated until the intended batch size is reached. Thus, we

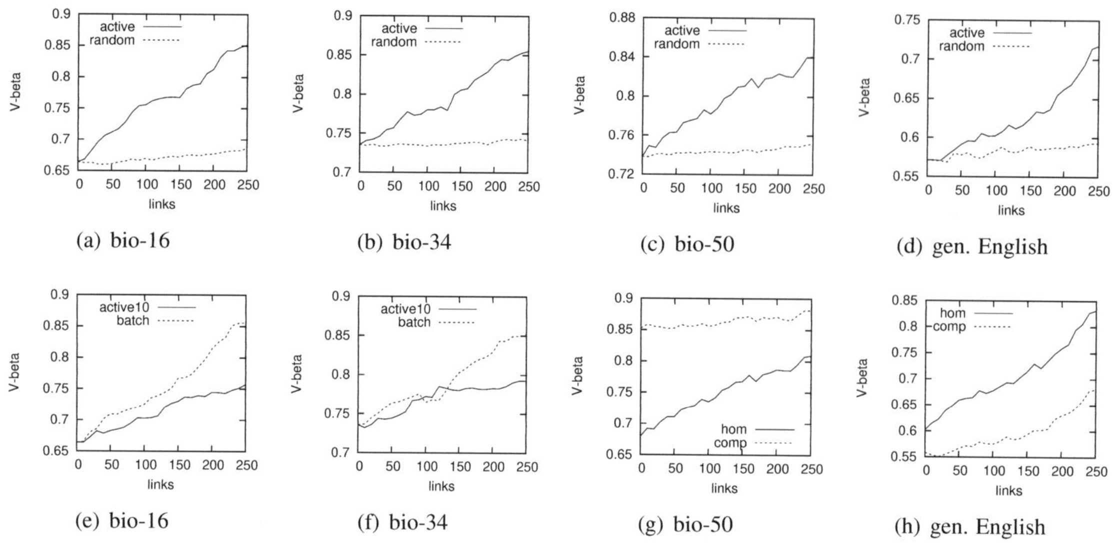

Figure 1: (a)-(d): Constrained DPMM learning curves comparing random selection and AL. (e),(f): Batch selection comparison. (g),(h): Homogeneity and completeness curves during AL.

avoid selecting links involving the same instance, unless their uncertainty was not reduced by the constraints added. A consideration that arises is that by reducing the number of samples used for uncertainty estimation, progressively we are left with fewer samples to rank the remaining links. Each labeled link reduces the number of samples approximately by half since the most uncertain link is likely to be a *must-link* in half the samples and a *cannot-lnk* in the remaining half. As a result, for a batch with size $|B|$ the uncertainty of the last link will be estimated using $|S|/2^{|B|-1}$ samples. A crude solution would be to generate enough samples for the desired batch size. However, obtaining a very large number of samples can be computationally expensive. Therefore, we set a threshold for the minimum number of samples to be used to estimate the link uncertainty and when it is reached, more samples are generated using the constraints selected. In graphs 1(e) and 1(f) we demonstrate the effectiveness of the batch selection method proposed (labeled "batch") compared to naive batch selection (labeled "active10").

6 Discussion and Future Work

We presented an AL method for constrained DPMMs employing uncertainty based sampling. We applied it to two different verb clustering datasets with 4 gold standards in total and obtained very good results compared to random selection. The idea, while explored in the context of verb clustering with the constrained DPMM, is likely to be applicable to other models that can incorporate *must-links* and *cannot-links* in MCMC sampling.

Most literature on AL for NLP considers supervised methods for classification or sequential tagging. However, AL for clustering is a relatively under-explored area. Klein et al. (2002) incorporated actively selected constraints in hierarchical agglomerative clustering. Basu et al. (2006) have applied AL to obtain *must-links* and *cannot-links* however, the clustering framework used requires the number of clusters to be known in advance which restricts counter-intuitively the clustering solutions that are discovered. Moreover, semi-supervised clustering is a form of semi-supervised learning and in this light, our approach is related to the work of Zhu et al. (2003).

With respect to the practical application of the AL method suggested, it is worth noting that in all our experiments the constraints were obtained for the respective gold standard of the dataset at question and consequently they are all consistent with each other. However, this assumption might not hold in case human experts are employed for the same purpose. In order to use such feedback in the framework suggested, it is necessary to filter the constraints provided in order to obtain a consistent subset. To this end, it would be interesting to investigate the potential of using "soft" constraints, i.e. constraints that are provided with relative confidence.

References

Sugato Basu, Mikhail Bilenko, Arindam Banerjee, and Raymond J. Mooney. 2006. Probabilistic semi-supervised clustering with constraints. In O. Chapelle, B. Schoelkopf, and A. Zien, editors, *Semi-Supervised Learning*, pages 73–102. MIT Press.

Ted Briscoe and John Carroll. 2002. Robust accurate statistical annotation of general text. In *Proceedings of the 3rd International Conference on Language Resources and Evaluation*, pages 1499–1504.

Trevor Cohn, Sharon Goldwater, and Phil Blunsom. 2009. Inducing compact but accurate tree-substitution grammars. In *Proceedings of Human Language Technologies: The 2009 Annual Conference of the North American Chapter of the Association for Computational Linguistics*, pages 548–556.

Hoa Trang Dang. 2004. *Investigations into the role of lexical semantics in word sense disambiguation*. Ph.D. thesis, University of Pennsylvania, Philadelphia, PA, USA.

Benjamin C. M. Fung, Ke Wang, and Martin Ester. 2003. Hierarchical document clustering using frequent itemsets. In *Proceedings of SIAM International Conference on Data Mining*, pages 59–70.

Dan Klein, Sepandar D. Kamvar, and Christopher D. Manning. 2002. From instance-level constraints to space-level constraints: Making the most of prior knowledge in data clustering. In *Proceedings of the Nineteenth International Conference on Machine Learning*, pages 307–314.

Anna Korhonen, Yuval Krymolowski, and Nigel Collier. 2006. Automatic classification of verbs in biomedical texts. In *Proceedings of the 21st International Conference on Computational Linguistics and 44th Annual Meeting of the Association for Computational Linguistics*, pages 345–352.

Beth Levin. 1993. *English Verb Classes and Alternations: a preliminary investigation*. University of Chicago Press, Chicago.

Chih-Jen Lin. 2007. Projected gradient methods for nonnegative matrix factorization. *Neural Compuation*, 19(10):2756–2779.

Marina Meilă. 2007. Comparing clusterings—an information based distance. *Journal of Multivariate Analysis*, 98(5):873–895.

Daniel J. Navarro, Thomas L. Griffiths, Mark Steyvers, and Michael D. Lee. 2006. Modeling individual differences using Dirichlet processes. *Journal of Mathematical Psychology*, 50(2):101–122, April.

Andrew Rosenberg and Julia Hirschberg. 2007. V-measure: A conditional entropy-based external cluster evaluation measure. In *Proceedings of the 2007 Joint Conference on Empirical Methods in Natural Language Processing and Computational Natural Language Learning*, pages 410–420.

Burr Settles. 2009. Active learning literature survey. Computer Sciences Technical Report 1648, University of Wisconsin–Madison.

Lin Sun, Anna Korhonen, and Yuval Krymolowski. 2008. Verb class discovery from rich syntactic data. In *Proceedings of the 9th International Conference on Intelligent Text Processing and Computational Linguistics*.

Robert S. Swier and Suzanne Stevenson. 2004. Unsupervised semantic role labelling. In *Proceedings of the 2004 Conference on Empirical Methods in Natural Language Processing*, pages 95–102.

Yee Whye Teh. 2006. A hierarchical Bayesian language model based on Pitman-Yor processes. In *Proceedings of the 21st International Conference on Computational Linguistics and 44th Annual Meeting of the Association for Computational Linguistics*, pages 985–992, Sydney, Australia, July.

Andreas Vlachos, Anna Korhonen, and Zoubin Ghahramani. 2009. Unsupervised and Constrained Dirichlet Process Mixture Models for Verb Clustering. In *Proceedings of the EACL workshop on GEometrical Models of Natural Language Semantics*.

Kiri Wagstaff and Claire Cardie. 2000. Clustering with instance-level constraints. In *Proceedings of the Seventeenth International Conference on Machine Learning*, pages 1103–1110.

Xiaojin Zhu, John Lafferty, and Zoubin Ghahramani. 2003. Combining Active Learning and Semi-Supervised Learning Using Gaussian Fields and Harmonic Functions. In *ICML workshop on The Continuum from Labeled to Unlabeled Data in Machine Learning and Data Mining*, pages 58–65.

Author Index

Briscoe, Ted, 57

Chrupala, Grzegorz, 27
Clarke, Daoud, 38
Croce, Danilo, 7

Daumé III, Hal, 51
Dinu, Georgiana, 27

Erk, Katrin, 17

Ghahramani, Zoubin, 57
Goyal, Amit, 51
Guevara, Emiliano, 33

Jagaralamudi, Jagadeesh, 51
Jurgens, David, 1

Lutz, Rudi, 38

Previtali, Daniele, 7

Stevens, Keith, 1

Venkatasubramanian, Suresh, 51
Vlachos, Andreas, 57

Washtell, Justin, 45
Weir, David, 38

Association for Computational Linguistics
209 N. Eighth Street
Stroudsburg, Pennsylvania 18360

CURRAN ASSOCIATES INC
proceedings
.com